Perpetua

Perpetua

The Woman, the Martyr

Sarah Ruden

· ANCIENT LIVES ·

Yale
UNIVERSITY PRESS
NEW HAVEN & LONDON

Copyright © 2025 by Sarah Ruden.
All rights reserved.
This book may not be reproduced, in whole or in part, including illustrations, in any form (beyond that copying permitted by Sections 107 and 108 of the U.S. Copyright Law and except by reviewers for the public press), without written permission from the publishers.

Yale University Press books may be purchased in quantity for educational, business, or promotional use. For information, please e-mail sales.press@yale.edu (U.S. office) or sales@yaleup.co.uk (U.K. office).

Frontispiece: Beehive Mapping.

Set in the Yale typeface designed by Matthew Carter, and Louize, designed by Matthieu Cortat, by Integrated Publishing Solutions.
Printed in the United States of America.

Library of Congress Control Number: 2024950799
ISBN 978-0-300-27371-7 (hardcover)

A catalogue record for this book is available from the British Library.

Authorized Representative in the EU: Easy Access System Europe, Mustamäe tee 50, 10621 Tallinn, Estonia, gpsr.requests@easproject.com.

10 9 8 7 6 5 4 3 2 1

· ANCIENT LIVES ·

Ancient Lives unfolds the stories of thinkers, writers, kings, queens, conquerors, and politicians from all parts of the ancient world. Readers will come to know these figures in fully human dimensions, complete with foibles and flaws, and will see that the issues they faced—political conflicts, constraints based in gender or race, tensions between the private and public self—have changed very little over the course of millennia.

James Romm
Series Editor

For herself, of course

Although we are unworthy to add anything to an account of such great glory, still, we will carry out what amounts to a testamentary injunction of the most holy Perpetua — or what is in fact her solemn charge.

—*The Suffering of the Holy Perpetua and Felicitas*

Contents

PREFACE xiii

Introduction 1

Chapter One. Born, Educated, Married 11

Chapter Two. Converging Forces 29

Chapter Three. Her Own Hand, Her Own Impressions 57

Chapter Four. I Knew I Spoke with the Master 81

Chapter Five. Fattened for a Sacrifice to Caesar 107

Chapter Six. A Picture with the Face Torn Out 135

THE SUFFERING OF THE HOLY PERPETUA AND FELICITAS 155

SOURCE NOTES 171

NOTES 175

INDEX 185

Preface

I come to Perpetua from several starting points—and I hope that does not remind readers of Stephen Leacock's Lord Ronald, who "flung himself from the room, flung himself upon his horse and rode madly off in all directions." I began my scholarly life as a translator of the Greek and Roman classics, then swerved into retranslating and commenting on the sacred literature of Christianity and Judaism. In the meantime, I ricocheted as a poet, investigative journalist, personal essayist, cultural historian, and book reviewer.

This book is a project that synthesizes classics, sacred literature, and women's literature. The work has been acutely tantalizing. The Christian martyr Perpetua is an author like those in the classical canon or the array of church fathers, with knowable (or surmisable) historical roots and a distinct voice. Yet she is not left alone to speak: her account of her break with her pagan father and her time in prison appears to have been edited and has a voluble third-party presenter and at least one coauthor, people who might be called controllers and competitors as much as admirers.

Even so, there is no hiding her jutting, sometimes jangling personality. She was on a proud and passionate quest to be herself, a person apart from her family and her narrow female roles, and for her this meant ceasing to be a person on earth: she was (almost) unwavering in the cause of self-annihilation for her faith, or martyrdom. Yet she had no interest in spiritual self-annihilation: she considered herself already powerful enough to pray her deceased brother out of a proto-purgatory, and she looked forward to being a celebrity in heaven. But to evaluate her thoughts and feelings in

Preface

the aggregate, not to mention her place in religious and cultural history, is a complicated business. Augustine, for instance, handled her popular legend with heady praise of her that was sometimes weakened by his doctrinal officiousness, reminding his congregation that her story was not canonical, not authoritative as scripture was; moreover, his prodding of certain passages into doctrinal shape is not necessarily something she would have minded. In her own words (or words in her diary that might have been altered or inserted after her death), she kept returning to meek piety after flights of self-assertion.

I have a new feeling about the little-known Perpetua: she does not need mere time, diligence, honesty, or even devotion from me. I suspect that she needs something more difficult, something like justice. It is easy to become transfixed by her fate as heroic and pitiable and to forget about the remarkable *person* who met it, a martyr like no other. I have tried to balance scrutiny, admiration, and sympathy in my assessment.

Most hearty thanks go out to the University of Pennsylvania Classics Department and to the university's libraries, especially to Rebecca Stuhr. And what can I tell you, my editors James Romm and Heather Gold, and my agent Gail Hochman? Without your patience, your hard work, and your faith in me, nothing happens here.

Perpetua

Introduction

The life of Vibia Perpetua provides an incomparable opportunity for thinking about the rise of Christianity, but she is also fascinating in herself. This young mother from a respected family was the star among a group of martyrs who died in the year 203 CE in an amphitheater near (or perhaps not so near) Carthage, the metropolis of a Roman imperial domain on the Mediterranean coast of Africa. Her social position made her fate noteworthy enough, but she also left a "prison diary." It is framed by the words of at least two other people, a Christian instructor named Saturus, who was a companion in her martyrdom and a fellow visionary (the fifth, final, and longest vision in the amalgamated document is his); another man who presented the entire document, adding his own portions (scholars call him the redactor, or rewrite man); and perhaps yet another narrator who witnessed the spectacle of the executions and provided oral or written news of it, which account winds up the story.

The collection, by pretty solid consensus the earliest and most authentic record of Perpetua's final days on earth, is called *The Suf-*

Perpetua

fering of the Holy Perpetua and Felicitas.[1] Felicitas, a slave woman who gave birth in prison, was the only other female member of the group. The text, though it aims at religious witness, is not sacred literature — or not the usual kind. Many threads of fact and probability attach the exposition to contemporary society, and nothing shown happening in Perpetua's world needs supernatural forces as an explanation. Moreover, the heroes of the story are limited and hapless enough to calm suspicion that the *Suffering* is an inspirational legend based on the transcript of their judicial hearing (or on a lot less). Most of the female martyrs of antiquity who, like Perpetua, later became saints of the Catholic church — figures like Agnes and Agatha — have only a Styrofoam anchor in history: their names and their deaths during persecutions may be real, but the rest of their stories sounds very much like the fantastical inventions of ancient Greek novels. For example, an angel strikes blind a man who approaches Agnes in the brothel to which the Roman authorities have consigned her as punishment for clinging to her faith and her virginity.

One obvious reason that the memory of such women could travel swiftly in male imaginative vehicles into the land of pious myth was that these women were not speakers or writers themselves. Perpetua *was* a writer, expressing herself "in her own hand" and "giving her own impressions," according to the redactor (and the majority of modern scholars back him up).[2] With tangible satisfaction, she conveys her defiance of her father, the loyalty she shows her fellow Christians, and, most of all, her assurance that she has made a righteous decision and will be rewarded for it.

Socrates, Perpetua, Dietrich Bonhoeffer — it is fascinating to hear (even if only indirectly) of martyrdom from its practitioners. The quirky humanity of the voices may be startling; our half-conscious impulse is to revise in the retelling in order to come up with some-

Introduction

thing more comfortable, something more on our own scale. But insight and exhilaration can come from facing up without flinching to the words of those who used their own bodies to break through the walls of a confining civilization.

In this respect, Perpetua is an informant of marvelous value. Her account is nothing like the mainly theological and moralistic writings of the church fathers, our main source about Christianity in the age following the composition of the New Testament books. The church fathers have plenty to say, but most of it is abstract, dominated by their otherworldly ideology, which did not leave much room for what we would call social-justice concerns. One such concern is equality. Although we may hear consistently from the modern media that Christianity in its earliest centuries throve as a relatively open and egalitarian movement, the reality included peculiarly Christian strains of authoritarianism, and especially of misogyny, for both of which Christianity's male leaders vouched ad nauseam in their writing. Through no mysterious motivations, female witnesses to their faith were reduced over time to sermon texts instead of people with their own backgrounds and points of view, and their own authority founded on their own sacrifices. Perpetua and Felicitas themselves became such rhetorical tools for Augustine, antiquity's greatest preacher.

There is also a relevant subcategory of early Christian literature, much of it collected by the late-third-/early-fourth-century church father and so-called father of church history Eusebius: accounts of martyrdom. Though these deserve more credence than medieval miracle tales, the conventions of the topic here (if not of the real events) tend to be narrow and stilted. A single witness — martyrdom — crowds out the mundane teachings of Christianity about fallibility, tolerance, and adaptability. The rhetoric — stern warnings about the devil's efforts to weaken the martyrs' resolve, for instance, and baroque images of blood — is employed indiscriminately over quite different situations. The action steps in existing footprints like a hiker trudging through deep snow; martyrs are horribly tortured yet impervious to pain, torturers and hostile crowds are overcome with awe. I hope I can be pardoned for noting that these dramas about judicial murder become more boring the more of them I read.

    The *Suffering* is, uniquely, not like these works; it is immediate and convincing, partly because it shows martyrs in their idealistic but very human relationships with one another and with those outside their circle, but chiefly because the leading participant and main narrator is so vivid. Perpetua is a brash newcomer to Christianity; the process of her martyrdom actually begins before her baptism. She has a convert's enthusiasm but does not show much interest in pious self-abnegation; instead, she relishes the prospect of her martyrdom as a pageant of self-fulfillment and manages her words and actions to worldly dramatic effect. As an author, she is utterly unlike (for example) Ignatius of Antioch, who composed pious letters during the journey to his execution in Rome sometime in the first half of the second century. She is also unlike modern literary martyrs, most of whom have been at pains to place their choice in a context of the metaphysics and ethics they believe made them who they are. Autobiographically, Perpetua comes out of nowhere, and she sounds like an immature recruit to self-sacrifice, no more an ideological leader than the average star of an army boot camp class. Besides the indulgent glorification she expects in heaven, she is preoccupied with family and material matters, and with the personal impressions she is making. However, she is audibly full of compunction about violating the conventions of martyrdom, with which she does seem to be familiar, and keeps batting down her own mental flights and (briefly) caging herself in edifying language and sentiments — *if* these are hers and not the redactor's. As to her be-

Introduction

havior, she appears to have tried mightily but not completely successfully to endure to the end in the way she was expected to.

No wonder Christians around her at the time—and not only those who came after her—intervened in her witness. One man nudged and flattered her into visions, and another probably came to act as a dream partner. In other ways too, she seems to be managed like a star performer. When she is first jailed and feeling overwhelmed by her hardships, a church official pays a bribe to move her, along with her companions, to more comfortable quarters. Perhaps with the help of further bribes, the group is paroled for a time, then allowed numerous visitors, then feasted like gladiators, who were the iconic celebrities of the games. The concessions could not all have escaped the notice of presiding pagan authorities; they might have agreed explicitly to at least some of them. Technically, professed Christians were enemies of society, like others awaiting public execution; their captors could have disposed of them in a few moments. But like the Christians who cried up martyrdom's power for recruitment, the persecutors had an interest in a riveting public drama, so in this case they needed to sustain enough of a genteel young woman's dignity to make their smashing of it impressive. Along with Perpetua's shortcomings as a representative of her religion, the evident serendipity between the interests of Christian and pagan leadership in her death is a realistically disturbing angle on her story.

But how much of the story is a chain of real events and reactions to them, and how much is narrative alone? The text is anything but a spontaneous outpouring; in forty years of studying ancient literature, which is full of adaptations, misrepresentations, and pure fancy, I have never seen an author so openly shoved to the side, shushed, and interrupted. The redactor, awkwardly, places much more conventional Christian language than hers around her writing, though he does show leanings toward the mystical, heretical, woman-friendly New Prophecy or Montanist movement.³ Worse, only eight of the twenty-one passages into which modern scholars have divided the *Suffering* were written by Perpetua, and the rest are so insistent on the party line of martyrdom, and so unlike her voice, that I picture her with a pillow pressed over her face. Even some of her own writing is excised, the most glaring instance being at the start of her narration. It is inconceivable that Perpetua herself in her draft or recitation did not give *any* answer to the questions that would be on everyone's mind: how and why, around the critical time when she produced her husband's heir, she turned to a suspect and despised religion in the company of at least two slaves, and how that religion came to trump all her other attachments and obligations. Again, her extant story does not begin until *after* her arrest; and it does not reach backward except when, prompted by a vision of the underworld, she tells how her young brother died years earlier.

As if these empty spaces did not frustrate the tantalized reader enough, modern scholarship itself, in its way, evinces a certain amount of suppression. So closely tied up is Perpetua's story with enduring sanctities of Western culture that researchers have not forthrightly and probingly assessed her personality or other likely influences on her momentous calling. She has had no real biography prior to this attempt of mine, even though, among other distinctions, she appears to be the first female prose author in Western history whose work we still possess.

This shortfall may be due less to how little is knowable about her, and more to how much. Tightly edited as the *Suffering* is, Perpetua's account of herself and others' accounts of her do characterize her vividly — too vividly for pious tastes, which is why she becomes little more than an icon in later tellings. In life, she was not

Introduction

only spoiled and self-centered, easily manipulated through her vanity by those who stood to benefit from her death. She was also gifted in ways the ancients did not admire in women — though adherents of the Montanist movement may have differed in this — or at least not when the gifts were in any way inconvenient to the men in their lives, or to other sources of male authority. She was clever, with a striking sense of gallows humor; and though her faith was steadfast, it was imaginative and individual: she did not simply accept whatever people told her about the unseen world, she *saw* it in marvelous detail.

But her full story has not proven a soothing Christian fable in any age, including our own. Her reception points to a problem beyond the straightforward restrictions on women speaking for themselves. The public sphere, where women are not supposed to be, tries to restrict them to expressing what is "feminine" when they do land there; their most consequential stances can thus serve men's most self-serving ideas about women.

The clearest quashing of the real Perpetua is her sanctification, her transformation into the Saint Perpetua who rises to God because she rises above her feeble womanhood. Her popular persona became stranded between the spiritual Good Cop and Bad Cop, Mary and Eve, a woman who comes to the rescue of humankind through her emptying out of will and self, and a woman who dooms humankind because she is led to doubt that God has made the best deal for her and her mate, and acts on her doubt. Yet the distortions are not only those of Late Antiquity and the Middle Ages. As an example of a crudely exploited persona, Perpetua reaches into the age of modern propaganda that began in the nineteenth century, and clear into the age of identity that began a few decades ago.

In an effort to face Perpetua more directly, I have made a new translation of the *Suffering* and based this biography on it. I include the translation in this volume so that readers can see my excerpts and citations in their full context and come as close to Perpetua's unmediated personality as I can point them. It was in reading her words and the surrounding words of her contemporaries concerning her that I realized how striking yet disconcerting a presence she must have had; at the same time, I could see how vulnerable she was to being manipulated in her life, and after her death written over and made to stand for causes, attitudes, and ideas that might have puzzled or repelled her.

Modern translations are certainly better than the wholesale rewritings and replacements that appeared earlier, but William Farina in his book on Perpetua provides a good summary by example of how slow and partial improvements have been. In the first English translation of the *Suffering* to be published, a Victorian one, the purported eyewitness writes that the spectators in the arena stare Perpetua down when she enters with her contingent. Farina then cites updates indicating that she stares *them* down, which is without question the sense of the Latin.[4] But these more recent translators retain a bland and misleading construction of the word *delicata*, used of Perpetua in the same sentence. Perpetua in the Latin is "Christ's wife," but also "God's *delicata*." The original word choice does *not* make her simply the "darling" or "beloved" of God, but the "alluring/charming/pleasing/ delightful/luxurious/voluptuous" one of God.[5] In literature, the word is used of spoiled and pampered favorites — as in fact Perpetua seems to have been to her father and to other men in her immediate world and in her visions. If she is in a *legitimate* metaphoric relationship to divinity, she is the expensive, coddled wife who has turned her husband's head and perilously centered the household on herself. The attitude she

Introduction

shows nearly everywhere seems to justify such disquieting irony in an otherwise flattering account of her.

This sentence sets a question lodged in the text in motion once again: What has happened to the man who made her an honored *matrona*, gave her a home, and fathered her baby? Edgy as a true rendering of the Latin *delicata* has to be, it is appropriate. Perpetua was out on the edge — though it is unclear exactly why — and must have made even her contemporary admirers nervous. Why would distancing sarcasm not break through? My choice for a translation is "the pampered darling of God."

I hope that my own rendering of the *Suffering* will help make this biography more directly answerable to the text's various voices. But this text is lamentably short and piecemeal. Political, social, and religious history have to suggest the young woman's fuller life, including her past and the thoughts that she did not trust to voice or paper. What I can know and guess about her is tantalizing rather than satisfying, but it begins to light up for me the turbulence and complexity of the early Christian world. The most fascinating person in it, I find, was in some ways bound to her time, yet in others timeless, in some ways extraordinary and in others readily recognizable: stubborn, impetuous, tender, quick-witted, blinkered, hungry for purpose — a credible self such as we find nowhere else in all of antiquity's accounts of women.

CHAPTER ONE

Born, Educated, Married

Vibia Perpetua offers some sharp challenges for a biographer, but they are irresistible. There is no doubt about her importance. She was one of those incandescent personalities who emerge to startle everyone around them: a born leader with an unbreakable will and a legacy that would be difficult to erase. But there is hardly a figure of comparable stature at such a late period as the early third century CE, and in such an important place as the Roman North African metropolis of Carthage, and in such a momentous movement as early Christianity, about whom we know so little.

Her sex no doubt added to her obscurity. With few exceptions, women in the ancient world were not considered full human beings to whom man-size stories should attach; they did not often act in the observable public sphere, thus putting themselves on record; and decorum required that their private lives remain private. In Perpetua's case, biographical obscurity would have had a religious dimension too. As a fervent early Christian, she would have denied that her time before her baptism, and particularly the time before the few weeks spent in prison and the hour or two in the arena, were much more than darkness, error, and the deathly flesh, out of which she was reborn to the true and eternal life of salvation. No wonder that, in her prison diary (unless these passages are now missing), she did not look back at her upbringing or studies or marriage or the birth of her child, or ahead except toward her own magnificent death and a flattering and delicious paradise. If not for the few comments of the redactor near the start of *The Suffering of the Holy Perpetua and Felicitas*, we would see only one substantial piece of her background clear up to the moment of her arrest, and that piece is closely related to her present religion: in section 7, she describes a brother's agonizing death years earlier because he now figures in her vision of a doleful afterlife for the unbaptized.

Here is how the redactor introduces her: "Another member of the group was Vibia Perpetua, who came from a respectable family, had a gentleman's education, and had entered a proper marriage. She had a mother and father and two brothers, one of whom was also under instruction for baptism, and a baby son she was still nursing. She was around twenty-two years old."[1] Few descriptions of a celebrated figure in the ancient world have teased modern scholars as much. I will lay out what is most convincing, what is questionable, and what is baffling in it, and discuss what I think all three suggest about Perpetua's life as a whole.

Her name certifies an at least partial Roman descent or enculturation, and seems at first to suggest high status. Lucius Marius Maximus Perpetuus Aurelianus (-*us* is a masculine Latin ending) was a Roman senator and her contemporary who held several high imperial offices; he was also a noted biographer. His family might have come from Africa, as they were certainly not old Roman senatorial nobility. But we cannot rely on the name Perpetua to tell us that her people were prominent, or that they had any connection to Rome that they knew about. The "no relation" disclaimer common where identical American surnames are concerned would have been useful in the sprawling Roman and assimilated populations.

"Perpetua" may sound like an acquired name alluding to the Christian idea of eternity, but mere serendipity was probably at work here: Perpetuus/Perpetua was plainly an existing Roman name, and in fact the word does not have to mean more than "long enduring." But perhaps one thing that early publicists of Perpetua seized on was that she had a name so suitable for a martyr. Another piece of nomenclature could hardly have been more favorable to pious messaging: her female companion, a slave, was called Felicitas, or, colloquially, "good luck" or "happiness." Felix (lucky, happy) was a common name for male slaves, so again there is no reason to assume thematic renaming, even though *felicitas* does have a religious meaning: "blessedness." *Perpetua felicitas* is wordplay that creeps into subsequent narratives of the episode and that Augustine uses repeatedly in preaching about the two martyrs around two hundred years later: the linkage of the names produces the meaning "eternal blessedness."[2]

"Vibia" is the *gens* name, identifying the whole family or clan. Roman girls traditionally used their fathers' gens names, feminized, as their own first names, with the cognomen ("with-name," at this period of history usually indicating a smaller division of the family) following it. Carthage was resettled as a Roman colony in the second half of the first century BCE, so it could be that Perpetua's first local ancestor dates from that time. At any rate, the family appears to have flourished. An excavation at Carthage revealed inscriptions with the names Perpetua and Vibia at the site of the Basilica Maiorum (Church of the Ancestors), where a fifth-century Christian source locates Perpetua's burial; but the key find is a broken sixth-century marble slab—purported to replace one destroyed by the Vandal conquest in the fifth century—memorializing Perpetua and her comrades. Her family may have owned the land (was it their own burial plot?) and built a conspicuous monument to her. But there is no historical record or sure archaeological sign of great wealth or political leadership among her close relations.

Rome had defeated and devastated the maritime commercial center of Carthage and the surrounding territory in 146 BCE, three and a half centuries before Perpetua's death. Romanization had inexorably redeveloped such a valuable piece of real estate, and the city now had a sophisticated grid layout, a world-class port, and monumental public buildings, all in the Roman style—and of course a Roman imperial administration. But the culture was not monolithically Roman. It accommodated not only people of Phoenician descent (Carthage had developed as a Phoenician colony before it came to Rome's attention as a rival) but also North African peoples who were closer to indigenous. British rule in India, South Africa, and so on is not a good template for thinking about exotic Roman provinces. The Romans were highly pragmatic, did not subscribe to anything like legal and "scientific" racism (through which modern nations have condemned whole groups to slavery or annihilation on the basis of their appearance and biological descent), and had considerable openness to other communities with which they felt they could amalgamate without any threat to public order. Jews and Christians were among the few cultures that at times stuck hard in the Roman imperial throat. There is no reason to picture Perpetua as racially Italian, as her family might have followed money and intermarried with locals—for example, with those whose ancestors had bought back property from conquering and confiscating Romans. Freed slaves even acquired Roman names from their former masters. But to picture her as black African, or (as the Romans put it) Ethiopian, would be stretching the probabilities. To

Born, Educated, Married

Mediterranean people, Ethiopians were rare and striking. According to the New Testament, the first man to convert to Christianity seems to have been instantly recognizable as an Ethiopian, and he is placed against his exotic background before anything else is written about him.[3] Could Perpetua have been an Ethiopian without exciting any comment to that effect?

As well as Phoenicians and indigenous peoples, there were Greeks, representing a way of life that flourished in many parts of the Roman Empire, including Alexandria at the mouth of the Nile. Perpetua does not display the linguistic snobbery you would expect from a well-bred Roman lady in Rome itself who had ventured into prose writing for public consumption. (The venture was not unheard of. Agrippina the Younger, for example, a member of the Julio-Claudian imperial dynasty, wrote about her own era, and the account was available to later historians.) While the Romans proper considered Greek essential for the kind of education that developed rhetorical skill and allowed a man to enter public life, they frowned on Greek words in formal Latin writing. But Perpetua does use Greek words, such as *fiala* for a drinking bowl.[4] Greek was probably an intimate and accepted language for her from long before the *Suffering*, not just known from texts that may have informed her conversion and encouraged her martyrdom. Her deceased brother had been called Dinocrates, a Greek name. Her fellow martyr Saturus envisioned her in paradise speaking Greek to two still-living leaders of the church to address their quarrel — that is, she speaks it outside her family and a sheltered, studious circle, and with confidence, perhaps to native speakers.[5] This suggests an eclectic, open, and stimulating environment.

More freedom and opportunity for Perpetua also would line up with the majority judgment of scholars concerning her social class — I return to this topic because class was determinative in the life of a young woman in the Roman Empire. She was not in the lofty and conspicuous position that would have kept her from the more footloose associations and activities that landed her in trouble. Truly aristocratic women dressed up, paraded in the right places (with entourages that helped ensure that they did not go off track), entertained the right people, and mated for dynastic purposes. The higher their rank, roughly speaking, the less likely they were to nurse their babies, whereas Perpetua nurses hers. She could be also nursing out of high-mindedness, but the authors who urged this focused on the welfare of the precious heir and future family representative, and Perpetua's baby, as I will show, was in a very different position.

But altogether, the *Suffering*'s summary of her background is not very helpful concerning her position in society. She is (literally, in the Latin) "respectably born," which can mean that her family was prominent. But the adjective from which the adverb "respectably" comes, *honestus* (with its obvious English derivative), does not pin the redactor down: in some contexts the English "solid" or "decent" or "our kind of people" is the sense of the Latin word. They cannot be feckless or needy or alien, but they do not have to be a great deal more.

Perpetua's family might not even have been metropolitan. Some Latin manuscripts and the Greek version of the *Suffering* locate Perpetua and her fellow Christians not in Carthage but in an outlying town, Thuburbo Minus. (The only previous known persecution of Christians in all of North Africa had occurred twenty-three years earlier in another town, Scillium, which was also in the same province as Carthage, Africa Proconsularis.) Scholars naturally want to place her father at some level of public service, because even minor provincial worthies, including freedmen who had made good in business, often held offices patterned after those of Rome and

Born, Educated, Married

Italian municipalities and formed the nodes on the vast web of Roman imperial power. In return for the prestige and connections these posts offered, men were expected to spend on public benefactions — particularly the handouts and shows that helped secure their own elections. To my mind, one logical difficulty in assuming that Perpetua belonged to one of Carthage's leading families is that if this were the case, her father would have been in a position to sponsor major public entertainments himself. How, then, could he not have personally known the organizers of the local birthday celebration for the emperor's son Geta — the games in which his own daughter died? Had he fallen out so outrageously with the regime that its revenge was, in a round-up of Christian nobodies (two of Perpetua's fellow prisoners are identified as slaves), to include the person he loved most in the world, his daughter, and not the son, who was also a Christian initiate?[6] But an ugly and implacable rift within the religiously divided family is a better possibility, as I argue below.

The biggest threat to the assumption that Perpetua belonged to the highest class is her father's treatment during a judicial proceeding by the Roman magistrate in charge of the province: while hearing her case and that of her friends, this official has an attendant throw the old man down and beat him, perhaps with one of the rods that stand for the power of physical punishment.[7] But this power was limited; to have a citizen beaten without even a hearing would have been a shocking breach of Roman legal norms. Moreover, the father has not done anything wrong except interrupt the proceedings; he is on the platform only to plead with his daughter — over whom he probably maintained absolute legal authority, though she had married (it took *manus,* literally "hand," a special legal provision, to transfer the father's power to the husband, and by this era, manus marriage was rare) — to renounce her Christianity and perform an idolatrous sacrifice for the well-being of the joint emperors, Severus and his eldest son, Caracalla.

Perpetua's father is urging exactly what the magistrate himself urges, in line with an imperial policy that dated from the reign of Trajan (98–117 CE) and was probably modified by a policy of Severus, that only those converting to Christianity and those who converted them should be punished, rather than all Christians who came before a magistrate and refused to renounce their religion. At any rate, a quick ritual offering, signifying pro forma that emperors were gods among other gods — something that many pagans themselves did not believe — and, more important, attesting to civic loyalty and conformity, would have gotten Perpetua off. But she would not do it. The fertile, respectable young matrona was a sine qua non of Roman civilization; there could be no patriarchy without such women to serve it. Yet this matrona had chosen to detonate herself. Her thoughts and feelings were not supposed to go beyond the tender, the dutiful, and the decorative, but they were fixed immovably on the prospect of her own defiant and triumphant death.

It is thus readily imaginable that the father and the magistrate connived to put extreme pressure on Perpetua. But if that is so, the father planned his own alarming degradation as an effort to retrieve a family member who owed him obedience but did not give it, who was publicly disgraced already, and, as a female, was more disposable than a male. This suggests an exceptional devotion on his part. Was she in so much trouble in the first place because he had never used against her the considerable power that went with being head of the household but rather let her make important decisions on her own? However it came about, he shares in her scandal now; he is probably right in asserting that her punishment will silence the family hereafter — that is, banish them from active public life.[8] If he cannot do something as basic and normally uncontested as control his own daughter — or, failing that, save her life — how will he and his sons not be laughingstocks in the eyes of the community?

Both male and female citizens were exempted from cruel and degrading punishments, so there arise questions about Perpetua's own treatment as well as her father's. Some of the historical context in which Christians are concerned is straightforward. In the biblical book of Acts and Pliny's letter to Trajan it appears that at an early period Christians who were Roman citizens took advantage of their legal immunities and exercised the right to appeal their case to the emperor in Rome. Later, when martyrdom was a movement and a deliberate spectacle, things became more complicated. Eusebius's *Church History* includes the purported original text of a letter from Christian assemblies in the neighboring cities of Vienne and Lyon, narrating a persecution the took place in the year 177, and this letter contains a wealth of detail about how public administrators handled Christians. Some of the Vienne and Lyon believers who were Roman citizens defied official attempts to spare them or at least to delay or lighten their punishment; they died of tortures as horrific and public as those inflicted on helpless Christian slaves. That Perpetua died alongside slaves and others clearly less privileged than she, and died by the same means, says a lot about her character and her exalted place in Christian memory, but it does not help us place her in a specific social class and civic status. If her social rank afforded her a way out of martyrdom in the arena, she rejected it.

Concerning Perpetua's marriage also, questions need to be posed within the historical context. *Matronaliter nupta*, which I translate as "had entered a proper marriage," is more or less untranslatable Latin. The words contain so much more than their commonsense modern meaning, which is that she did not merely live with her partner but was a *wife*, sanctioned by paperwork and a ceremony. The Romans recognized several kinds of domestic partnerships, with different (and mostly loose) rules. However, it was not mainly legalities but social and material arrangements that created a matrona. Perpetua (or the Perpetua of the text) had had a sheltered upbringing that guaranteed her virginity until marriage, her match was made through careful negotiations between the two families, she had a substantial dowry that her husband would have to pay back if the marriage did not work out, and in public she wore a veil (*nupta,* "married," literally means "veiled") and a special modest dress, long enough to lap over her feet. A series of laws enacted starting from the late first century BCE sought to mandate marriage and fertility for a girl of her class and threatened dire punishments if she were unfaithful; the laws were not effectively enforced, but they portrayed her as the heart of the home and the linchpin of community stability.

I do not doubt that Perpetua was a matrona. How, except from a careful upbringing, could she have gotten her education? A family in difficult circumstances or outside the mainstream might see the rationale for educating a promising son — but a daughter? For what purpose? Sheltered cultivation, the only kind for a respectable girl, would have been absurd where there was no intimate cultivated circle to appreciate it. Would the family have been training up a high-class entertainer (i.e., a sex worker who could offer more than sex to educated gentlemen)? Slave owners and managers of the demimonde might do this, but not married parents; their decency, and any standing they had, was bound up with raising their daughters for marriage (or, in extremis, keeping them at home). The stress on Perpetua's having a regular, visible *family,* with all the familiar components (father, mother, brothers), amounts to an insistence that she was not a concubine and not an independent woman but had had a recognized marriage. She in fact has a devoted father and a mother and brother willing to help her with her baby.[9] It would seem difficult, if these people had never existed, to conjure them into a story with so much verisimilitude overall. If they did exist, they could only signify that she was — or started out as — respectable.

Her apparent single status would not in itself have destroyed her respectability. Divorce was permitted among pagans, and fairly common. It even had a certain cachet, because women with high status, and larger dowries to claim back, could go through a divorce with less worry about their futures. And because marriage was an institution organized mainly for building bridges between families and breeding heirs, not for companionship or romance, the bond between spouses tended not to rival close friendships or blood ties. It is not surprising that Perpetua's husband or ex-husband is never mentioned; he may have simply removed himself from her troubles and aspirations, to his family's satisfaction.

Or Perpetua or the Christian editor may well have erased any involvement he did have; his very existence is, after all, a problem. Female martyrs were much more conveniently presented as virgins. In the legends, they sustain their virginity through obstacle courses of pressures and atrocities, and die in a state of equal purity and dispensability. The defection of an established wife as a martyr was another matter, though apparently not so much within the Montanist or New Prophecy movement, two of whose founding leaders were women who left their husbands. But that had been decades ago and a world away (in what is now Turkey), and would not have been easy to explain to the kind of communities depicted in the New Testament, with house churches run by one patriarchal family each and aiming at stability and decorum clear down the social scale of members. The apostle Paul had decreed that Christians must not divorce even pagan spouses if these were willing to stay.[10] And the entire time the cult of virginity was developing, only the most fragile and suspect strains of Christianity authorized the wholesale abandonment of a marriage, as opposed to an unconsummated marriage, something that Paul did not envisage but that some Christian leaders came to treat with enthusiasm, no doubt in part because without children, family fortunes could go to the church.

In any event, whether Perpetua's husband pleaded with her, was outraged, or simply gave up in the face of her overriding devotion to her Christian cause, he would have been a demoralizing figure for her coreligionists and potential converts to contemplate, and a warning to pagans viewing Christianity from a distance. It may even be that the marriage broke down for a reason other than religion, and this would reflect worse on her among Christians: she would have lost her marital home (the wife had to leave) not from spiritual devotion but for some cause that a pagan woman might also cite (if she were not too embarrassed over it). These speculations, of course, all assume that he was alive. But if she were a widow, why does she (or the editor) not say so? Chaste widowhood was an honored state in the eyes of both pagans and Christians.

What throws all these possibilities into confusion is the status of her baby. By law and custom, it belonged to the husband or, if he were dead, to his family; she had no rights to it whatsoever. I can imagine an ex-husband or ex-in-laws leaving her to finish nursing it if the marriage ended, but Perpetua is first seen starving it through her absence in jail, and then keeping it with her in the jail's squalid, confined, and dangerous quarters, from which she is released only temporarily. Eventually, her own father refuses to give her baby back to her.

Did some or all of the parties scramble to make some humane arrangement in this emergency, regardless of who owned the baby? Roman law did not in reality have the stringency or formality we would suppose if we relied on the digests compiled in Late Antiquity. Legal faits accomplis are rife in the historical record. The law comprised a grand and orderly intellectual system, but the English Common Law that the United States inherited is even grander and more orderly, yet the claim that American society can depend on it to prevent or punish all heinous acts should give rise to sardonic hoots. The *Suffering*, like ordinary people's correspondence on papyrus excavated and studied over the past couple of centuries, seems to show that people used to getting their way paid no attention to the law. I can easily believe, for example, that the imperial Roman official presiding over the hearing of Perpetua and her companions did not worry for a moment about having a provincial citizen beaten. What was anybody going to do about it?

As to the fate of Perpetua's baby, something truly curious is going on, because the situation is not in its basis a matter of law but rather of custom — the things people are accustomed to do. There is a reason for the ancient saying "Custom is king." In historical time Roman men owned their children by law because, long before any law was written down, they had acted as if they owned their children, and woe to anyone who disputed that right. Perpetua's husband or ex-husband or his family had the customary power to take the baby; he or they did not exercise that power, either declining to — an extraordinary choice at the time — or being prevented by some momentous factor.

A husband did have the option of either raising a baby or abandoning it to death or enslavement, but by custom this was a decision made immediately after the birth. Perpetua's baby outgrows breastfeeding in the course of the story: he might be one or two years old or older. Strictly according to the law, a father could treat his child almost any way he chose at any stage of its life, but after its earliest infancy only dire circumstances could have impelled him simply to turn his back on it. By agreeing to raise the child, he had made it part of his household, his public standing, his future, himself. If the father died, his family would step in to preserve his interests in continuity that they shared. Yet in the *Suffering,* Perpetua and her family dispose of the baby, presumably an only son, without interference. It is hard to guess how the boy is going to fit into a Roman community outside the norms of either legitimate birth or adoption. The baby's putatively uncertain status and prospects suggest, at the least, far more than the average rift between families during a Roman marital breakdown.

I do not share what may be some readers' extreme discomfort with the idea that a woman who was wholeheartedly religious and committed to self-sacrifice might still find herself with a huge personal mess on her hands, a mess that at least in part is her own fault. Institutional religion and determined heroes of it may be skillful at covering up such messes, but modern biography testifies that they can happen. Thomas Merton sounds perfectly sincere in recalling his desire to become a silent, ascetic monk instead of a relatively comfortable Franciscan, and he did join a Trappist monastery and remain in the order for the rest of his life. But he had also begotten an illegitimate child during his student days, which hardly made him look like the ideal prospect for a novice a few years later, and during middle age he fell passionately in love. From my own experience of "intentional" religious communities, I would hazard that an utter mess made of personal life is the rule, not the exception, for spiritual strivers, and that if the rules were strictly applied, these places would be empty.

One good starting point for intuiting what went wrong in Perpetua's private life is another phrase in the editor's description of her: *liberaliter instituta,* literally "educated freely" or "educated for freedom." In my translation, I write "a gentleman's education";[11] it certainly is not "a liberal arts education," such as might be certified by a humanities degree from Williams College, nor is it a "gentlewoman's education." The Romans meant an education fit for a boy who was freeborn and more specifically one who would not be busy earning his subsistence but could aim to distinguish himself in public business: this required, above all, a thorough training in oratory. Such an education would have been unthinkable for Perpetua as a woman, and what she evidently did achieve—vivid, direct, confident communication—likely led to conflict and frustration in the adult life for which she was destined.

Many women were literate; some enjoyed Greek and Roman literature, the basis of rhetorical study. But no woman of Perpetua's time had any approved use for oratory, the usual projection of a full education into self-expression. Women had been banned from acting as legal advocates since the early first century BCE, and had always been shut out of the policy-making sphere. Perpetua is not conventionally eloquent. She mixes in Greek words with her Latin and does not use a full repertoire of standard prose rhythms; polished oratory was in this and other ways like poetry in traditional forms: it demanded intricate craftsmanship. She could have learned the skills she displays by listening to her brothers practicing beginners' declamations.

I do not agree with the exponents of Perpetua who claim that she had studied philosophy, the crown of a Roman education; their main evidence appears to be that she insists to her father that she has to be called what she is, a Christian, just as the pitcher she points out has to be called a pitcher.[12] This looks like an appeal to common sense, not to Aristotle's *Metaphysics*. I am reminded of a quip attributed to Abraham Lincoln: "How many legs does a dog have if you call his tail a leg? Four. Saying that a tail is a leg doesn't make it a leg." He was not extemporizing on the philosophy of identity but instead, with earthy wit, demanding respect for reality at a time of crisis. Perpetua is doing something similar, asserting the reality and vitality of her commitment: it is as solid as a physical object, and as adhesive as that object's name. If she had any abstract erudition, she does a magician's job of hiding it throughout the part of the *Suffering* she wrote.

Perpetua's voice reminds me most of Anne Frank's. Frank was also her father's favorite, and also drew on a sheltered upbringing and limited reading to respond naturally, movingly, and idealistically, if narrowly, to a looming threat to her own life. Both women were born for a privileged female fate but instead fell headlong, though with a strange degree of self-possession, into history. Perhaps both Frank and Perpetua met the first real resistance in their lives in the form of a sprawling, ruthless state; it does not seem as real to them as the protectiveness of their own intimate circles.

But Perpetua is wildly different from Anne Frank, and from every other author, in her very awkward blend of ingenuousness, celebrity self-presentation, and cooperation with all those who were exploiting her suffering and death as performance art.

In short, we have no here-to-there narrative for Perpetua, from the indulgent and stimulating family home to the vestibule of death. But the genteel Roman girl's corridor to early marriage, with no doors on either side, implies a great deal, which can be pictured along with the redactor's outline of Perpetua's life and the story of her martyrdom. I am certain that she did not shine like the sun in her husband's universe, as she had in her father's; hers would have been a Roman marriage in a million if she had found in it praise for her mind and spirit and encouragement to pursue a demanding religious vocation. Given the confinement and close supervision typical for young girls, it is likely she came across this religion when she was already married, if not already a mother. And given the usual position of men as spiritual and social leaders of their households, it is unlikely that her husband approved of her conversion, much less that he was willing to follow her into the lowly and vulnerable Christian community. Whether bad feeling between Perpetua and her husband spurred her to look for stimulation and approval among Christians, or whether the marriage was doing well until she met Christians, her new commitment could hardly have brought the partners closer. That her own family members were (at least according to her) all Christian except her father, the patriarch who had endorsed and probably arranged the marriage, may have made her situation worse.[13] It was altogether a scene set for bitter, household-dissolving conflict.

CHAPTER TWO

Converging Forces

The conditions under which Imperial Roman girls from substantial families lived must have played havoc with their development. I find it remarkable that so many eventually arrived at tombs that testified to the deep grief of their families, and in some cases to their status as pure and selfless *univirae* or "one-man-ers." These women did not remarry even if they were widowed young — which often happened, as menarche qualified a girl for marriage and childbirth at an age at which her brother would be perhaps only halfway through his education. But perhaps — and Perpetua's story supports this — few women managed to meet the demands on them gracefully. Perhaps the whole range of funerary homage is a cover for the kinds of matronly perverts, clowns, and psychopaths that Juvenal parades in *Satires* 6 (an account extreme in its bitterness but with all its major themes endorsed by more moderate writers). Women, after all, faced steep psychic challenges even in the kindest of homes.

Ironically, one set of challenges could arise from a father's self-centered idolization of his young daughter. This happened in an emotional landscape that was otherwise bleak even for extremely privileged girls and women, so the contrast between this relationship and others would have been trying. Infanticide, which picked off more girls than boys, left concentrated female targets of paternal regard, and brighter and more appealing daughters in particular must have had a schizophrenic time of it. A number grew up as their fathers' adored darlings, the sweeter and more tractable versions of the boys; but they were exiled into marriage as teenagers, and hardly found the same treatment thereafter. Their sexual initiation was notoriously traumatic, and in their new homes they tended to get more attention from waspish in-laws than from their husbands. In *Satires* 6 Juvenal has nothing critical to say about marriageable girls except to predict that if a destined bride seems perfect, she is going to look down on her husband, which will be unbearable to him.[1] A young consort, plainly, could do no right. But at this stage she was (if she was lucky) playing her most important role in life, bearing the requisite small number of children. What about later, when she was more dispensable?

Perpetua's father is not ashamed to say he devoted himself to her upbringing, favoring her over all her brothers.[2] She is self-confident and sharp-witted, and could not have grown up that way without her father's encouragement. Around the age of twenty-one, she is a *matrona* with a baby son, but no other signs of her marriage are found in the text. It is a thorny-looking outcome.

A letter of Pliny the Younger from about a century earlier, concerning the death of a friend's daughter, gives an idea of what might have been Perpetua's upbringing (though readers will have to allow for differences besides those of time: Pliny's circle was near the top of Roman society, right under the emperor).

Converging Forces

In the deepest grief I write to you, now that our friend Fundanus's younger daughter is dead. I have never seen anything more joyful or lovable than this girl, anything that didn't deserve not just a longer life but—almost—immortality. She had not yet finished her fourteenth year, and already she had the wisdom of an old woman, the seriousness of a proper wife, but at the same time the sweetness of a girl along with a virgin's shyness. How she used to cling to her father's neck! How lovingly yet modestly she embraced her father's friends! How fond she was of her caretakers, her minders, her teachers for every duty they fulfilled toward her! How carefully, how intelligently she would read aloud! How restrained she was in playing, and how grudging in spending time this way! With what self-control, what submission, with what perseverance she endured her final illness! She obeyed the doctors punctiliously, tried to cheer up her father and her sister, and kept herself going with her sheer strength of mind when her body's strength had abandoned her. This strength of mind held out to the last, and was broken neither by the length of the illness nor by the fear of death. Hence she left us more and heavier reasons to miss her and grieve for her.

What a truly sad and painful demise! What timing, which she deserved less than the death itself! She had already been appointed for an excellent young man, the day for the wedding had already been chosen, we had all already been invited. What joy transformed into what grief! I cannot describe in words the wound that my heart received when I heard—I was right there—Fundanus (because this is how a painful loss turns up a great many things to lament) giving instructions that the money that he was going to spend on clothing, pearls, and gemstones be used to buy funerary incense, ointments, and spices. He is in fact a learned and wise man who dedicated himself from his earliest youth to the loftier studies and practices. But now he rejects everything he often heard and said, and with all his other noble traits driven out, his devoted love is all that remains in him. You will forgive him, even praise him, if you consider what he has lost. He lost a daughter who was an exact copy of her father in every respect, with an amazing similarity, reproducing his ethics as well as his looks.[3]

According to the ancient system of reckoning ages, the girl Pliny describes was actually not yet thirteen, instead of under fourteen; this was the age at which the father was willing to marry off his paragon. Notice also that the author—according to the etiquette of the time—does not give her a name, or at least not in the published version of his letter. Her public identity is a sort of penumbra of her father (after whom she would have been named according to custom, with "the Younger" because her sister was older), obscured within his household. Worse, she had a social tightrope to walk, but he did not. Whereas she showed ideal courage and patience clear up to her death, in his case the key philosophical and moral principle of not indulging in inordinate grief has—quite understandably, according to Pliny—broken down after this perfect feminine counterpart of himself vanished.

Pliny and Fundanus do not care enough about the girl, as a human being analogous to themselves, to reflect on what a letdown most of her life to follow would have been had she recovered. A young matrona like Perpetua, who had done her duty by producing a healthy male heir and now saw ahead of her no mission of equal importance, would be lonely, frustrated, and aggrieved in proportion to the seriousness of her former studies, the impressiveness of her character, and above all the regard she used to enjoy. For the Romans, a well-developed self did not count if you could not show it off, and where could a wife have found an amenable audience? According to Juvenal, the woman discussing current events with male acquaintances in public, her husband standing silent beside her, was a monster of bad manners.[4] But what (besides frivolity and mischief) was a mature woman to aspire to, if she could not even let her opinions be known? Would she have been happy working wool among her maids late into the night, like Lucretia in Livy's *From the Founding of the City*—a winsome sight for her husband and his drunken friends to drop in on, should they chance to have made a bet about what their wives were doing?[5] Lucretia, the perfect victim as well as the perfect wife, is raped within a few hours of this scene, and kills herself, despite the pleas of her husband and his friends, in order not to suggest to any woman defiled through her own doing that a claim of rape is a way to escape the death penalty. At some point, the Roman version of acceptable womanhood starts to look to me like a fool's paradise, and the adventure of independent choices like a good gamble.

No wonder, therefore, that Christianity appealed particularly to a woman like Perpetua. The assembly (a worship, teaching, and social gathering) of Paul's time in the first century CE had allowed women to speak on an almost equal basis, and although that right fell away from the mainstream church later, the New Prophesy movement—which at Carthage gained the first literary Christian superstar, Tertullian, as a sympathizer—fostered it, sharing out authority that male elders (today's priests) and overseers (bishops) had been holding exclusively. The redactor of the *Suffering* echoes words from the New Testament, which in turn echo the Hebrew Bible, to certify both men and women as epochal witnesses to God's will: "'In the last days,' says the Master, 'I will pour out my Spirit onto everyone alive, and their sons and daughters will speak out; and on my slaves, both men and women, I will pour out my Spirit.'"[6]

But all sects of Christianity showed a refreshing interest in their followers' understanding of what they had signed up for, and the boldness, complexity, variability, and controversy of Christian doctrine from its start provided either a satisfying exercise for their minds or, if they were passive thinkers, an intellectual spectacle. From the mid-first century, when Paul the missionary locked horns with both sponsors and rivals in Jerusalem and abroad, there were almost as many Christianities as leaders and locales. Some, from our point of view, were Christian only by a straining stretch; Manichaeanism looks more like a vegan cult with a mythology as wild as Scientology's. Especially before the famous unifying conferences and fixed creeds that began in the early fourth century, women and other previously excluded people could enjoy Christian polemics in the same way male citizens enjoyed the rhetorical contests of civic life. Christianity even had an entry barrier that encouraged informed and committed engagement. For men and women both, the indoctrination demanded in the catechumenate, or preparation for baptism, could last several years. With the apocalypse expected any day, eternal fate was supposed to hang on being right, even about abstract matters, and acting on it.

Perhaps most appealing, especially for women, in the Christian movement were calls to action. The church wanted its members to solidify one another's commitment, impress and shame the church's opponents, and draw converts, despite the difficulties imposed on a suspect and sometimes persecuted sect. Perpetua, though she was a woman, was encouraged to do far more than listen to sermons. With support, she could publicly enact the ultimate Christian mission of her time, martyrdom.

I am reminded of the way the First and Second World Wars drew many women into urgent public concerns and activities. A few generations earlier, respectable women were not supposed to go near the front lines; now they went by the thousands, and some were wounded or killed or taken prisoner. Martyrdom, the "testimony" or "witness" with the highest stakes during the first centuries of

Christianity, was one in which both sexes could participate; indeed, it was a heroism in which women could rise to prominence, with their own names, their own words before magistrates, and their own stories rivaling men's, long after the hammer of Christian misogyny had come down on them.

It was a heavy and stunning blow. After Paul's relatively mild decrees in his mid-first-century letters, the early-second-century pseudo-Pauline Pastoral Epistles condemned women to "salvation through childbearing," confinement to their homes (they were not even supposed to visit and speak with other women), and menial service.[7] Soon afterward, the church fathers began to have their searing say about women not only as answerable for the sin of Eve and the fall of humankind but as embodied evil; women were indicted with such ferocity that a reader might think the devil could hang all his crimes on them and walk free. But according to the Vienne and Lyon account, a Christian slave woman named Blandina wore out her torturers. She was the star of the persecution for this reason, memorialized in the letter about it that circulated among Christian congregations. Near at hand to Perpetua, five out of the twelve martyrs from the town of Scillium who died in 180 were women.

Though Christians ended up imitating, and exacerbating, pagan repression of women wherever they could, the simplicity of the standard legal process against suspected Christians allowed women an equal voice in court. There was no room for elaborate defense speeches (which no women were trained to give anyway), and in fact nothing was required for condemnation but a resolute confession of Christianity and the refusal to make a pagan offering. Women who proved as brave as men in confessing and enduring the consequences earned their own fame. And the sado-sexual interest in women in the arena could make women the higher-stakes, more thrilling victims, imprinted more deeply on the memory and imagination.

This was important, as martyrdom was not only a witness; it could be a spectacle. In some places it appears to have been a craze. Records of persecutions make clear that, however sincere and meaningful the choice to die for faith could be, at least the larger-scale incidents partook of social contagion. In the *Suffering*, Saturus turns himself in, joining other Christians in jail. In his dream, he meets three people outside this group who have already died "in this same persecution," and in another scene of the dream meets "many brothers there, and even martyrs."[8] This persecution might be a more important episode than it appears at first, even granting that probably no surviving record of it other than the *Suffering* is anywhere near contemporary. For the sake of comparison, the Lyon-Vienne persecution, called cataclysmic, enters extant history through a single letter that circulated among churches, a letter that happened to come to the hand of the much later historian Eusebius. But scholars simply need to make the most of the evidence they have when they evaluate martyrdom; to demand elaborate documentation in this field would be self-defeating, as if evolutionary biologists decided to make no deductions without a much fuller fossil record, perhaps including the mutant winged lizard that could not manage to fly and kept falling on its head until it was trampled by a giant herbivore.

That said, the Lyon-Vienne letter overflows with claims that point to acute social contagion, which is both natural in certain kinds of groups and fomented by those who stand to benefit from it. Loyal fervor for martyrdom generated more loyal fervor, with intellectuals supplying the exalted language while activists liaised with and supported those in prison and circulated news. Martyrdom became a sort of industry, aimed at enlarging and aggrandizing the community. Whether martyrdom did readily and directly inspire conversions from noble emulation, as depicted in the *Suffering* and elsewhere, is uncertain. But inducing followers to make extreme sacrifices can be an effective organizational move, and not just a proof of the leaders' existing power. People have a natural confidence in receiving in some decent proportion to what they give – kindness and affection in exchange for the same, trust in exchange for honesty, subsistence in exchange for work, and so on – so the promise of eternal life in bliss in return for torture and death would not have sounded outrageous. And to command that level of visible commitment showed Christianity as potent indeed.

The pressure for martyrdom can look merciless. The Christian hierarchy, and possibly Christian peers too, shamed and almost literally demonized those who threatened to retreat. Only the devil and his recruits could make them waver, whereas the opportunity to be martyred was a joy and a blessing, an invitation to heaven and a chance to be lionized in memory no matter one's character or circumstances on earth. Numbers of the Lyon and Vienne martyrs reportedly stood up to the authorities and went to their deaths only on a repeated try, obviously under emotional duress. Martyrdom, as imaged by a ladder to heaven in one of Perpetua's dream visions,[9] was a strictly one-way proposition; once in the authorities' hands and facing the most dire consequences of Christianity, a martyr must not turn back. Of course, to someone naturally brave who was longing to be admired and taken seriously, turning back was never an appealing option.

Young people show a stronger propensity for social contagion. Scholars have to depend on the late and unreliable *Augustan History* concerning the decree by the emperor Septimius Severus, who reigned during Perpetua's time. But it is plausible that if the decree existed, it was formulated as reported, for *containment* of the movement, with a prohibition on Jews and Christians *proselytizing:* only converts and converters were targeted. The martyrs shown being arrested in the *Suffering* are a woman around twenty-one who was under instruction for baptism and a small group of her classmates who are also *adulescentes* (usually meaning young adults); later their teacher turns himself in too. A difference in legal liability would, by the way, put the participation of church officials and other Christians in a more equivocal light than the text would at first suggest. The martyrs' visitors, advisers, and material supporters who act openly and without apparent fear invite the suspicion that they are making what we might call cannon fodder out of susceptible people; but they might also be seen as helping the only people the new law targeted. However, in yet another view of this same situation, the leaders would have been encouraging victims from a position of safety, safety that a little effort of their own in proselytizing would have done away with.

In any case, young people, with their paucity of experience and headier sense of the future, are more prone to reckless behavior, and more prone still if they are doing something together. As with social media today, they are an ideal target for older marketers who shield their own children from the same lures. And the prominence of the celibate among the martyred points to a hard fact: patriarchy, householding, and social position prevailed over holy risk. That was for those who had fewer responsibilities and less to lose, like slaves (Revocatus and Felicitas in the *Suffering*) and freed people, the virgins of legend, and a young wife at odds with her husband and family. In defense of Christian leaders in Perpetua's time, this was still the age of the house church as the center of the Christian community. (It took roughly another century for Christians to acquire large buildings for religious purposes alone.) The loss of the householder was a great loss indeed. But then again, Christian practices that prevailed much earlier, like shared property and official roles for women, would have mitigated such a loss and allowed more of the religious establishment to put their money where their mouths were.

As for young people, as if to facilitate their forays — the ultimate being martyrdom — into more-active and more-involved affirmations of meaning than the larger culture allowed, Christianity even supplied an ideological tool to separate themselves from the most controlling and arbitrary figure in their lives, their father (or other male head of the household), who enforced the rules and could instantly pull them out of the self-expressive possibilities of an education and confront them with adult responsibilities of his choosing. This tool was the cult of virginity and celibacy. Paul had recommended marriage as the second-best option for those who needed a sanctioned sexual outlet, but his rationale for preferring celibacy was only that men and women alike were happier and more carefree in undistracted religious devotion.[10] By Perpetua's era, Greek philosophical idealism churning together with Pauline Christianity was cementing the thinking that there were two classes of Christians: the ethereally pure, with their affinity to God, and the earthbound and sullied, easy victims of the devil.

But — critically for a Christian in Perpetua's position — the male authors urging this were for many generations, and at the levels both of inherited realities and of present needs, playing games. Marriage, the old, ordinary sort, was the usual basis of belonging to a community, and not only for church officials who hosted gatherings in their homes. There was no orderly or safe calling to celibacy for individuals. And monastic organizations (this is something of a contradiction in terms: the ancestor of our word *monastic* originally denoted the solitude of hermits who performed wild stunts of ascetic self-denial) developed very slowly: the first order under church auspices was the Augustinians, starting in the early fifth century.

Earlier, a freeborn young person who opted not to marry would be hard put to it to belong in any town or city. The men could at least travel, accept hospitality, and work outside the home in relative safety — not that their presence tended to go over well; unattached male Christians, Paul being the first example whose doings are known in detail, struggled to make themselves useful and accepted, and did a lot of quarreling and moving on. An unattached girl or woman, someone who had broken with the parents who expected to marry her off or the husband (pagan or not) to whom Christian scripture decreed she must stay married, or the betrothed who alone was authorized to back out of the commitment, would be in sorry straits.[11] Fellow Christians would see in her nothing but trouble; there is no record of provisions made for young women who chose celibacy until, much later than Perpetua's time, those with extraordinary resources began to make arrangements for themselves. Destitute and homeless widows could act as servants of other Christians or apply for local Christian doles if they did not remarry. But there is no comparison between measures intended to keep hapless women from prostitution and tolerance of a woman who had arguably brought her misfortunes on herself; for her, the choice of heroic chastity was not something social realities could allow in the long term. Perpetua, I submit, went to the arena in part because she had nowhere else to go.

The process of Perpetua's alienation is not hard to trace in detail through the text of the *Suffering*. As the narrative opens, she has apparently not returned to her parents' home, as a respectable woman should do after her marriage breaks down or ends. She is in some other dwelling place with the same group ("we") who will accompany her to prison, if not with others as well, apparently in "free custody," a form of house arrest. The alternative to her being away from home is that the whole group is in a separate part of her parents' house, where her father visits her and from which he departs, but this seems absurd: why would he let the strangers with their disastrous influence stay with his precious daughter in his own home? I think that as a refuge her marital home is also a nonstarter. Brides went to live in their husbands' homes and had no right to stay if the marriage failed. Could Perpetua's husband, not even mentioned in the story and very likely out of her life, be hosting her and her friends while they are under house arrest?

Her companions in martyrdom are several unrelated Christians, male and female, including at least two slaves who are behaving as if they, and not their owners, are entitled to dispose of their bodies and their lives. (Perhaps they have a Christian owner or owners sanctioning their choice; the Lyon-Vienne martyr Blandina was a slave with an apparently Christian owner.) Perpetua's father is trying desperately to reclaim her, meeting a daughter's rebuffs that have no precedent in extant Roman social history.

> While we were still with our attendants, (she says), and my father wanted to turn my resolve upside down with his talk and wouldn't leave off trying to bring me down, because he felt so strongly for me, I said, "Father, do you see—just to give an example—that container lying there, a little pitcher or whatever it is?" And he told me, "Yes." And I told him, "It can't be called by any other name than what it is, can it?" And he said, "No." "It's the same way with me. I can't say that I'm anything other than what I am, a Christian." Then my father, reacting to this word, threw himself at me to tear my eyes out, but he only roughed me up, and he went away defeated, along with the arguments the devil had given him. For the next few days when I didn't

Perpetua

have my father around, I thanked the Master, and it was heavenly for me that *he* was gone. In this actual interval of a few days, we were baptized. And the Spirit told me that I was to pray for nothing from that water but to hold out against my body's suffering.

Perpetua does not invite her father to join her in conversion; she does not ask him to approve her determination to martyr herself, though she claims later that the rest of her family approves of it.[12] She coldly quizzes him by a simple example to the effect that her identity is fixed and controlling and has nothing to do with who he is to her or what he wants. She will die as a martyr as surely as the pitcher holds and dispenses liquid. Filled with rage at her defiance, he roughs her up—his right as a father, though he may never have exercised it before. Alternately, if his previous relationship with her was *too* controlling in any way, they may be going through the stage in which the child steps away and turns on the overbearing parent a face of immovable rage. Whatever their bond in the past, he will keep trying to restore it, applying hostage taking, flattery, and other manipulations, but nothing will work: whatever mechanisms may have served him before are useless.

For now, she belittles the attack ("he only roughed me up"), though (*pace* previous translations) the verb for what he does short of gouging at her eyes often refers to violence and can be used for harrying a battle line. That he has merely "vexed" or upset her is very unlikely in the context: though she later expresses pity for him in conventional words, *she* is always the one in emotional control during their encounters.

After this first recorded confrontation, she focuses again on words (in which she excels), instead of dwelling on the sudden violence, as she would do if she felt her body were an essential part of her being that must naturally draw her thoughts and feelings after it. She associates her father's efforts at dissuasion with God's and humankind's enemy, the supernatural liar and (literal) "slanderer," the devil; he was, axiomatically, behind all attempts to deter Christians from martyrdom, but especially rationalization. As an additional strengthening advantage, she commands the place where she is, and her father has to withdraw.

For a student of Greek and Roman culture like myself to read of a real young woman who had been brought up in it thanking a divinity for her father's absence and expressing her satisfaction over it is chilling. Such a loveless daughter in mythology would be a murderous traitor, her former, normal self rendered unrecognizable by some depraved passion. It makes emotional sense that Perpetua surrenders any idea of her life continuing after she has made this tremendous break. After narrating it, she avers that she can expect nothing from (or after?) her baptism but suffering and death.

Her second recorded meeting with her father is even more chilling. He visits her, probably in the citadel jail (he is described as "climbing" to it). He tries to extort her by telling of his past devotion and present misery, her threat to the family's standing, and her baby's peril in her absence; he brings tears and extravagant flattery to bear.[13] Though she writes that his suffering pains her, she adds a cold and manipulative remark about it: he is not happy for her, as the rest of the family is. And her words of purported comfort to him are a preachy dismissal of his patriarchal rights as well as of her own right to live if God wills otherwise: God's will is going to be done in court; his is the power, not theirs any longer. Her father leaves, crushed with sorrow. Notably, he does nothing to help her materially, perhaps believing that her hardships will wear her down. Church officials, however, have already bribed the group out of the sweltering general population, where they are subject to harassment and extortion, and into more salubrious quarters, though this is for only a few hours; naturally, the bribe takers would eke out better treatment in order to keep the money coming, and in larger sums. That is probably how the prisoners got a temporary furlough. But they all go back into the prison later, and at one point are in the stocks.[14]

With regard to her baby son, the narrative has already touched on (but mainly skirted) some troubling signs of a woman teetering on the edge of society, with her religious resolve maintained at great cost. Perpetua has reported terrible anxiety about the child, and during the furlough she caught up with his nursing—he had been starving, she reports—and made arrangements for his care with her mother and one brother. This may imply that before this she left the baby with someone who did not have the basic resources or the willingness to care for him, which is hair-raising, since wet-nursing or feeding infants with animals' milk was not an unusual or difficult expedient. The many newborns discarded through exposure and picked up by slave dealers needed, and got, substitutes for their mothers' breasts. Had the baby been lying disregarded, or only sporadically attended to, in a corner of the place from which Perpetua and her friends were arrested? Did his grandmother have charge of him and deliberately neglect him, or did she exaggerate the state he was in, putting her own version of pressure on her daughter? Or was Perpetua herself panicking about how her son was doing without her, hence her (literal) "failing because of not eating" to describe the trouble he is having with a mere switch in feeding habits?[15]

In any event, the deal made for the baby's care in the grandparents' home does not appear to hold. His mother remains anxious, but a new solution she brings about is a grim-sounding one: she and the baby will stay in the jail together. She declares that this takes away all her debility and suffering and her worry over the baby, so that the jail becomes a palace for her, her favorite place in the world.[16] But the situation is hard for me to accept as the family's free, unextorted choice of what to do with the baby, and I take with a whole bucket of salt Perpetua's stated joy over the results. In what sense was she happy, with her child sharing the prison conditions?

Some hard facts are worth considering here. Roman jails throbbed with noise, and they stank. On the evidence of what seems to be the best-preserved jail, the Tullianum in Rome, they did not have proper latrines or cooking or heating or bathing facilities or ventilation or good sources of light — any of the amenities that people enjoyed in shared places (like public baths and commercial eateries) if they lacked them in their own homes. The main part of the Tullianum consists of two large cells, or rather dungeons, one on top of the other. We know that on first entering prison, the appalled Perpetua is plunged in darkness, swelters, and is victimized by the general population before bribes secure temporary better quarters.[17] There is plenty of evidence that Roman prisons could contain smaller cells, but these would not have provided much privacy, or any protection from the jail's employees. Felicitas must labor and give birth under the eyes of a sneering guard.[18] Then, of course, there are the chains and stocks.

Exposure to physical abuse was the norm. Torture itself was part of the judicial process: people in vulnerable ranks of society were routinely interrogated under torture in criminal prosecutions. In persecutions of Christians, where officials urged the accused to renounce their "superstition" and save their lives, rough treatment could have passed as an attempt to help them. It also may be that sometimes jail staff simply got out of control. The letter concerning the martyrs of Lyon and Vienne recalls mere guards in the jail using the rack and killing a great many prisoners through strangling or suffocation.[19] But even if prisoners perished at the guards' hands, the account here is probably a mythic exaggeration: as I discuss later on, Christian prisoners were an economic resource; for them to have been destroyed wholesale makes no sense.

The authoritative Christian insistence that suffering for the faith was a privilege worked toward depriving victims of the relief of complaining; perhaps a remonstrance from above is the reason Perpetua's words of dismay are all in her first passage, and also the reason she mentions the stocks only in passing, setting the scene for the vision in section 8. Tertullian's *To the Martyrs* opens with a passage about the triviality of prison hardships for Christian prisoners: not only do fellow Christians bring supplies, but the darkness of the sinful world outside is greater, more criminality is out there(!), the prison stench is countered by the prisoners' odor of sanctity, and so on. The Lyon-Vienne letter keeps asserting that one prisoner or another felt no pain under torture. The *Suffering* does not include palaver of this specific kind, but the etiquette demanding displays of joyful gratitude for the gift of martyrdom as a guarantee of heaven results in huge gaps in plausibility. As far as the text itself is a performance, it breathes desperate pride but also psychic strain and division.

At the group's judicial hearing, Perpetua's father appears with the baby—he has control over it now—from among the excited crowd as she takes the stand last of her companions. He pleads with her for mercy for the child, a plea the magistrate echoes. He then endures a beating that does not move her, though she writes of shared pain and compassion for his wretchedness in his old age. The sentence of death by wild animals in the arena imposed on her and the other Christians renders them cheerful as they depart. Subsequently, she decides she wants the baby with her again in the prison, on the grounds that he was used to nursing from her and staying with her there, but her father refuses this request from her emissary, the Christian assistant or "deacon" Pomponius. She does not dwell on the separation, adducing that the baby was weaned and her mastitis cured according to God's will.[20]

Close to the day of the games, Perpetua's father comes to her a final time, one of the many visits allowed by a military adjutant, who has become awed by the Christian prisoners. The father's self-abasement is similar to his earlier behavior; his gestures include those of mourning (he tears at his beard), and his pleas are such as "could have moved every living thing God made" — but not Perpetua. Her last comment about him is brief and trite: "I was pained at his unhappy old age."[21]

Perpetua's most passionate human concern is for her brother, who has been dead for a number of years. Through the barrier between worlds she strives to help him, and receives a vision showing that she has succeeded: he will benefit from her intervention eternally in the eternal realm, in a joyful, unending childhood.[22] Her earthly relationships have all been harshly rejected, greatly distanced, or strictly sublimated. This should not be surprising. She has scorned the "flesh" to the radical degree that Christian preachers and writers urge — but hardly in idealized tableaus; rather, in ways that speak to her being, in every sense, out on the edge.

Hers was a doubly sealed fate because of something that scholars and popular writers have been slow to touch on: the humiliations of a passage through the judicial system for unprotected persons seized on women with special force, squeezing down who they were and what they could do, though their condition was far from ideal in the first place.

Arrest, imprisonment, and abuse in the arena would not only have sorely tried aspirations to transcendence, along with the basic sense of self and social connectedness, in either a man or a woman; there would also have been more horror for a woman, and especially for a sheltered young woman. She might endure pain and the prospect of death high-mindedly, but she could not avoid an acute female degradation, which to the Roman mind was a moral fact that went with physical ones. Christianity itself would take many centuries to begin reifying the principle that what counted was the will to be pure, and not what happened outside a woman's control. The *Suffering* veils the inevitable outrages, and in parallel to the virgin martyr fairy tales implies that Perpetua and Felicitas's modesty (to say nothing of their female bodily integrity) was always vindicated. In the arena, the crowd objects to the sight of the two women naked except for the nets that confine them, so the nets are replaced with loose tunics.[23] There might indeed have been a reprieve in this instance, but the text never concedes what is indisputable: for a woman, to be in these circumstances at all was to be at the mercy of entitled sexual sadism, which continued to loom even when it lowered its weapons. This tragedy should be more touching, and more significant, than the sanctimonious fantasies we inherit as part of the old martyr tales. What decent person thinks less of Joan of Arc in the face of modern historians' contention that she was probably raped in prison and suffered a breakdown, and that this is the reason she could no longer put up a determined and impressive defense in court? The likely facts should only make her more sympathetic.

In Perpetua's case, signs of the breakdown of the functional self start to register early in the *Suffering*. She goes from a house arrest with "attendants" to a jail whose terrors and discomforts she raises a lament about—not at all the prescribed reaction for a martyr. She mentions what I translate as the soldiers "shaking us down," but the rare expression is literally about violent shaking, often shaking something until it falls to pieces.[24] The further story provides evidence that guilt, shame, terror, loneliness, and despair were not absent from her martyrdom.

Converging Forces

One unusual piece of literature, a story probably entirely or almost entirely invented, allows oblique but hard-nosed commentary about what happened to Perpetua, and why, and how she handled it. *The Acts of Paul and Thecla* is a mid-second-century tale about a first-century woman, a purported contemporary and follower of Paul and in fact the first woman said to have been thrown to wild animals in the arena for her Christianity. (The anachronism is glaring. The *Acts* presents established machinery for processing an accused Christian through an accusation, a hearing, and an execution as an integrated part of arena games: it was generations after Paul's death that anything like this went on.)

The *Acts* strongly resembles Greek romantic novels, with their magical and fantasy elements, but this is a *Christian* daydream. What would it take, the story of Thecla in effect asks, for a female Christian convert of stout heart and sharp mind to get what she deserves, on earth and not just in heaven?

The claims inherent in the story as to how an independent and exposed female witness for Christianity can, with propriety and even safety, navigate the social realities of the Roman Empire are as ridiculous as anything in the later virgin martyr fairy tales — but the *Acts* is especially ridiculous in its tinny resonances of female frustration and rage, and not in a contrived blankness or denial concerning female degradation, as in those tales — and as in the *Suffering*. It is plausible that women had something to do with shaping and spreading the story of Thecla. There is no good evidence that Perpetua knew it, but that does not matter. On one level, she lived — and died from — its bizarre contradictions, which are all drawn from reality.

In a provincial imperial town (Iconium, in what is now Turkey),

Thecla is a beautiful virgin with an overbearing mother and a ruthless husband-to-be. The mother is apparently a widow; the girl does not have a father whose near-absolute power she must defy to follow Christianity, whose doting love she must reject, and whose public standing she will destroy. The widowed mother of a daughter on the edge of functional adulthood did not enjoy the benefit of the doubt she would in modern society, one reason being that she lacked the authority to deal on her daughter's behalf. Legal responsibility for the girl reverted to a guardian, normally a blood relation of her father. This mother, in her connivance with an unscrupulous younger man, is like an evil, meddling stepmother (already a well-established character in mythology and folklore), who deserves whatever bad consequences redound on her. In Vergil's *Aeneid,* the princess Lavinia's mother, Amata, who rebels against her husband's change of marital plans for her daughter out of skin-crawling fondness for her first prospective son-in-law, and who spreads chaos and death through her intransigence, is a much closer parallel than our idea of the parent with the superior nurturing and protective instincts built in and lasting a lifetime.

The sheltered virgin daughter, on the other hand, got every benefit of the doubt in such a scenario, as the natural victim, in dire peril once she lacks her father's protection. And since she has no power, she has no dependents at her mercy; she can hardly do much harm when she cannot leave the house alone and has no privacy within it. By the same token, however, she cannot take up independent, active heroism without denaturing herself and forfeiting all credibility. To return to the *Aeneid* as the lodestar for what is proper, the warrior virgin Camilla is a gallant and sympathetic character, but only because her father trained her with weapons from the time she could walk. Lavinia, innocent object of two powerful men's rivalry, not only does not utter a word throughout the epic; she does not *move* of her own volition, even when she is on fire.

So how would Thecla, an unmarried girl from a good family, fit into a story of conversion and mission? How can she even learn about a new sect propagated through meetings in private houses in the evening, let alone go out and do this sect's work? Any behavior indicating that she means to make her own choices about her future would ruin her reputation, and then she might as well not be a virgin any longer; she would be a sullied outcast, unfit to represent any group, movement, or idea.

Whereas the editor of *The Suffering of the Holy Perpetua and Felicitas* appears to cut away the untellable scenes of the main protagonist's fall from her social position as a young married mother, fiction allows for far-fetched invention in getting around comparable limits on a marriageable girl. The author of *The Acts of Paul and Thecla* has Thecla listening at her window (somehow, no one outside can see her) to the apostle Paul's preaching in a nearby house, where he is a guest. He is, against uncanny odds, in the right place to convert her even though she cannot come near him. He is unseen, holding a discreet meeting, yet audible to the neighbors, which makes nonsense of the precautions Christians took from early on with their assemblies.

With apparent envy, Thecla watches women (mature married women and widows, that is) entering the house. Under the power of Paul's voice, she falls into a holy trance of devotion; she has been taken completely out of herself and so does not bear any blame for not responding to her alarmed mother and betrothed; much less does she argue, defy, or turn a smug or indifferent face to their pleas.

The author, however, is hard put to it to shore up the impression of her passivity and innocence once she bribes her father's gatekeeper with jewelry in order to escape her house by night, then bribes the jailer with a silver mirror to gain access to Paul, who has now been thrown into jail through the connivance of her betrothed. She sits at Paul's feet and kisses his chains, oblivious to how this must appear to others, particularly in that sordid environment, or how the news of the encounter might be received in the town at large.

The author does not wholly gloss over the outrage and horror these acts would have called forth in the kind of society he knew. This fictional Paul is arrested for the offense of inciting women to celibacy. And when Thecla begs to travel with him, he himself recoils, telling her that this will cause trouble. She is, moreover, mistaken in expecting his adherence and help when, having followed him against his wishes, she falls into sexual peril: at that point, he abandons her. Modern readers tend to take Paul's reaction as a feminist criticism of the apostle as a hypocrite and a traitor to the young woman whom he has enticed, by extolling virginity, to opt for a life like his. But this view overlooks how (for one) it would have looked for a man like Paul to have a beautiful adolescent female protégée. (The closest role was that of camp follower.)

The narrative skates close to depicting Thecla as her community at large would have seen her: a renegade and ruined girl whose own father could, would, and should have had her killed had he survived to exercise his proper authority over her. To make her seem more sympathetic, her cruel mother must be the one who demands that she be burned as an example (whereas Paul is only scourged and thrown out of Iconium as a troublemaker who lures girls away from marriage). As the tale unfolds, the author must more and more relentlessly come to the rescue of Thecla's freakish and dangerous exposure outside her home. When she is led out naked to be burned, the governor weeps instead of counting her degradation as necessary and a fait accompli; she is saved by a miraculous downpour that quenches the flames. Another governor, after she begs only to remain pure, places her not in jail but in the custody of a kind widow who has lost her own daughter. Thecla prays her hostess's daughter into eternal life, much as Perpetua prays her long-deceased little brother into paradise.[25] The sight of her imperiled and naked in the arena moves the women in the audience to outrage, which reminds me of the piteous sight of Perpetua and Felicitas nude in a net and about to be offered to a vicious cow, and the audience's demand that they be clothed again.[26]

But with regard to Thecla's most dramatic deliverances, her story could not be less like that of Perpetua. Thecla emerges from the arena completely and miraculously untouched. The lioness will not hurt her, even when she is tied to it. A pit full of ferocious seals serves as baptismal water, the creatures are killed by lightning from heaven, and smoke from the resulting fire conceals her nakedness. Wild beasts kill each other instead of her. The fire used to goad bulls into tearing her apart consumes the ropes that tie her to them. The upset of the women spectators, the impression that the girl's foster mother is already dying of grief and shock, the pleas of a repentant would-be kidnapper of Thecla, and holy awe cause the governor to halt the proceedings and release the girl with praise. She finds Paul again, reports her triumphs, and returns home to her mother, proud and independent (her fiancé has died); she then continues as an active and influential Christian. In one ending of the story, she has many adventures as a hermit in a cave, as well as a healer and teacher, with noble ladies as adherents. A realistic threat arrives — a gang of assailants — but she escapes by entering into the rock of the cave. The other, shorter ending has her traveling through the rock to Rome to see Paul, learning that he has died, and being buried near him.

Perpetua lived; her story happened. It is the editing down of her text, the inclusion of her visions and other people's testimony, and her own selective reporting of real events, not concocted miracles and far-fetched exceptions to social norms, that keep the message where its sources want it: to testify to Christianity in public is worth any price, and the process, however painful and violent, is never ugly or shameful.

Sex, of course, had the greatest disruptive potential in the literature of martyrdom. It defies credibility that there was no sexual abuse of martyrs, but for Christians to report it as explicit fact would have broken the spell, registering that their sacrifices were not pure and spotless, that God had allowed their integrity to be blighted in this essential way, that Jesus their exemplar had been crucified, like everyone else, with his genitals bare and open to prodding, stoning, and snide comments. Logically, the code of silence only redoubled the converts' vulnerability, as it does for modern targets of sexual abuse who do not dare taint and alienate themselves by making their plight known. This glossing over was more urgent for women, whose sexual integrity was more than a characteristic of them; it practically *was* them: a pure *virgo,* or unmarried girl, like the legendary Thecla, a chaste matrona like Perpetua – or, negatively, a slave woman whose body was literally up for grabs, someone like Felicitas, who can be shown giving birth in the semi-public space of a jail. Presumably, Perpetua would have helped and comforted her if she were allowed, but she does not appear in this episode at all.

As a palimpsest of human limitations, heroic legends can be depressing. But even granting the extent to which Perpetua was a

Converging Forces

prisoner both of dreams about what women could overcome and of all the things that prevented women from overcoming them, I draw a surprising elation from her account of herself and others' accounts of her. She was too much alive, too vivid to become entirely the vehicle of a cause, even a cause of her own choosing, and she sustained her individuality even as she shot toward the end of her life.

CHAPTER THREE

Her Own Hand, Her Own Impressions

If the main narrator's style in *The Suffering of the Holy Perpetua and Felicitas* is arresting but not odd to our ear, it is because, centuries before modern writers thought they were inventing it, she had the intimate literary voice down flawlessly:

> After a few days, we were taken in at the jail, and I was terrified, because I'd never been anywhere that dark before. Oh, what a hard day! The heat was overwhelming because of the mobs of people there, and the soldiers were shaking us down. On top of all that, while there I was sick with anxiety about my baby. Then Tertius and Pomponius, blessed ministers who were looking after us, arranged by a certain consideration for us to be allowed into a better part of the jail for a few hours so that we could get some relief. Then we all went out of the prison and could do what we wanted for a while. I nursed my baby, who by this time was weak from not eating. I was worried about him, and I spoke to my mother and encouraged my brother, and I entrusted the baby to them.[1]

This hardly represents the norm in ancient writing. *Intertextuality* is the thrilling name scholars have given to the way Greek and Roman authors made each other's work their own. They spun off, they varied competitively — and they did it within literary forms that were either shared over long periods (such as the hexameter verse of epic) or derivative (such as biography growing out of earlier forms of prose).

Among the Romans especially, traditional rhetorical schooling nurtured this self-conscious interweaving. In the classroom, apprentice orators drew on a great variety of literature as models. They tried to add their own panache to shopworn topics, but the closest thing to origination sanctioned by their training was *inventio,* the "finding" of suitable *angles,* and the guide for finding them was not supposed to be the drive for self-expression, but other people's successes. How had Cicero gotten this or that client off this or that charge? How had he worked on the prejudices of the Senate to defend public order in a time of crisis? Of course, Latin writing spanned many genres and could be wildly flexible and imaginative, but it had been kleptomaniac on purpose ever since it began plundering Greek material to build a Latin library from the ground up.

Authoritative Christianity did not reject conventional rhetorical training or its results, as the church fathers and other educated believers evince; Perpetua's own contemporary and countryman Tertullian raised the Christian treatise to new argumentative and exhortative heights, and he did it by Cicero's method: he sounded like everybody else, only more so.

I doubt the ancients would have understood our everyday cultural paradox that the personal is political, which makes the intimate and individual a possible subject for art of public stature. Authors were always nominally describing human experience, but they put a thick layer of emulative, traditional forms between their selves and their audiences. It sometimes seems as if they do more to distract from reality than to probe it. A Latin novelist of the mid-second century whom I have translated, Apuleius, could not have written an un-scintillating sentence without having a nervous breakdown, whether he was dilating about ethics or rotten cabbage, religion or sex with a donkey. I do not think much of critical efforts to find allegory or other deep meaning in his story: to me, the style is plainly the point.

The steady grind toward more refinement and sparkle over the centuries by no means ruled out simple, colloquial, or even crude writing; every style, every register was a self-conscious choice and a demand for readers' aesthetic appreciation. Julius Caesar wrote a treatise on the precise kind of plain and highly accessible Latin he used in his speeches and war memoirs. The fragments of Petronius's *Satyricon*, offering farce, obscenity, and long stretches of Vulgar Latin, open with a high-flown rant against decadent rhetoric.

In lyric poetry, where we would most confidently look for the unrhetorical—for spontaneity, for emotion, for confidences—our anachronistic expectations hoodwink us. *Lyric* meant "performed to the lyre": it was the poetry sung at banquets, and also danced to and chanted ritually in public in honor of the gods. The troupe of girls or boys trained for a festival were not there to say how they felt. Women authors, because they were women, were confined almost entirely to this highly formal and performative genre, and they were not taken seriously if they used it for self-expression. Though Sappho describes in the feminine first person a seizure of silent, jealous passion for a woman who is talking to a man, the ancient world's greatest literary critic, whose work comes to us under the name Longinus, treats the poem as an artifice, not as a record of something that happened: Sappho, he gushes, creates a lofty effect by a list of reactions that is superbly well deployed; realism as we would understand it is not something he looks for or would sanction, especially in a scene like this one.² Women were accorded the literary role of faking it.

But Perpetua bypasses language as a costume, and goes some way toward making writing the imprint of a life. In this, she has one pagan counterpart, the Roman emperor Marcus Aurelius, whose *Meditations* were titled literally, in Greek, "the things for himself." But he was a philosopher, concerned mainly with placing experience within intellectual frameworks. Perpetua sounds as if she is right in the middle of things.

Her affect and style testify to an indulgent though limited education at home. Evidently no one pushed her expression into any of the categories of rhetorical precedent or fashion; and nobody else's words had taken deep root in her in the way that helps develop even modern writers who are pledged to originality. She is not like a literary disciple: not traditional, not institutional, not collegial, and not emulative. She is just strikingly herself on paper.

Nor does she use the mundane modes of typical business or family letters. Like the other voices in the *Suffering*, she speaks to the world at large. The preface writer even classes this testimony with scripture, and perhaps above scripture as a rescuing message for Christians during the last days before the apocalypse. The Christian Bible (including Hebrew scripture, widely available in a Greek translation—but the whole was not a fixed or commonly available collection in Perpetua's time) did differ hugely from the writings of Christian intellectuals. Like Perpetua's style (and also that of Saturus), it can be called subliterary, but there the resemblance ends: most of it is repetitious, formulaic, and relatively impersonal. Individuals act and speak, but most of them are shown either carrying out or opposing God's will in fairly flat terms, rather than revealing their own inner lives and relationships in detail. Later books of the Bible, especially among the Apocrypha writings (appended to the so-called Old Testament but written in Greek), can show substantial Greek pagan influences and so have more personality. The book of Tobit is like a holy novel or adventure story. *The Shepherd of Hermas* and the *Apocalypse of Peter,* works of the apostolic fathers period (of Christian writers whose lives were said to have overlapped with those of Jesus's apostles), contain individual prophetic visions in considerable detail, as the *Suffering* does. Such works jostled for ranking with what we call scripture. But if the *Suffering* did so too, it was not *like* scripture; I doubt that the redactor would have claimed it was. It is far too fresh and immediate.

Odds are that Perpetua had never been bookish, and the fact that she died young increases those odds. My surmise is in line with prevailing household realities of her day even for boys. The era had arrived of the portable, easy-to-store codex, the book in modern form with pages and front and back covers, which was replacing the scroll. Rich people owned a lot of books, some metropolises had important public libraries, and booksellers offered popular titles and had texts copied to order by literate slaves. But this did not mean that young people were allowed to choose books, read on their own, or develop their own tastes. Children lucky enough to be schooled spent a great deal of time doing exercises on tablets and reciting their lessons, the boys eventually composing to strict standards and performing out loud for a teacher's stringent ears. Parents frowned on school-age children of either sex playing when they could be doing something productive; private time or space or recreational reading, thinking, or scribbling—the recourse to a "room of one's own" that Virginia Woolf called vital for nurturing an independent sensibility—is not something I have found any evidence of in that culture. The Roman habit of reading to oneself out loud would have militated against this anyway: to read for their own purposes,

Romans had to command their environment in ways young people could not. Roman boys of the leisured class might find their way eventually to literary freedom with the help of friends and patrons out in the world. But what hope for that did their sisters have?

So how did Perpetua land in her sometimes naive-sounding but wholly competent and confident mode of expression? Her narration sings with alertness, intelligence, and self-possession, and its abrupt start, which is very likely the redactor's mutilation, is the main fault in its structure. Perpetua's own contribution to the *Suffering* is the work of someone used to communicating, used to being listened to.

Her father's efforts to cultivate her could explain that experience at home: he was delighted with her lively mind but did not prod her toward intellectual or professional goals. What could these have been? But the gatherings of Christian communities explain how she found a semi-public but not overly critical forum for her thoughts. The assemblies of "brothers and sisters" had borrowed from Jewish synagogues their rare openness and intellectual ferment. Second Temple Judaism's practices are notoriously poorly documented; what went on in Christian assemblies is known as if in glimpses and overheard phrases; but everything that *is* known points toward discussion, discovery, and rediscovery. The obscure Jesus is shown not only taking up the role of teacher at will but also interpreting scripture to declare himself the Messiah. Writing of one early Christian assembly, Paul slaps his forehead over its freewheeling goings-on: people are speaking in tongues without any interpretation.[3]

The term for an individual's testimony in the assembly is one that scholars tend to translate as "prophecy," but in Greek it is closer to "speaking out" or "making a [privileged] announcement." Our word *prophecy* tends to connote prediction because outspoken figures as early as the first Hebrew prophets had so much to say about the future; later Jewish apocalyptic thinking turned into a lively expectation of the apocalypse among early Christians. For example, Paul takes the trouble to calm anxieties that an assembly has generated concerning those who die before the end of the world, when the faithful will be taken to heaven.[4]

The end of historical time was a special concern of the Montanist movement, which started around the middle of the second century, when the mainstream of Christianity had stopped counting on the imminent apocalypse and was turning to other issues. If Perpetua was in fact influenced by Montanism — perhaps above all by its prophesying women — this puts an interesting cast on the directness and urgency of her writing. Martyrdom was, as the *Suffering's* redactor makes clear, supposed to be a key witness as the end of time approached, and that witness spread through writing like this very text. And Perpetua does give the sense of tightly linking what she did and what she wrote.

One instance is her way of dealing with her agonized worry about her unbaptized brother, who died a number of years earlier. She does not keep her worry to herself, or speak privately with a man about it, though women are told in Christian scripture to take questions that arise for them in the assembly home for their husbands to answer.[5] She writes up the whole story in this new document, which is destined to be published. But first, she creates the story through action. She has had a vision about the problem: Dinocrates is trapped in a sort of proto-purgatory. She prays on her own authority for a solution, and she has a vision of the solution: God has made Dinocrates joyful and carefree, drinking from a gold vessel and playing in the water in a sort of childish baptism. In the best New Prophecy manner (at least as scholars reconstruct it from the late and scanty evidence), she has taken care of everything through direct revelation and bold ministry, though she is a woman and so not conventionally learned or eloquent. Her concerns are extremely ambitious, but they are narrow, in line with her sheltered and confined life. The book of Revelation was the scriptural touchstone for the New Prophecy movement, but I think that the movement's women, particularly, found their own ways of communicating.

None of this commentary of mine gets to the heart of Perpetua's writing. If a pampered girl's education at home and a religious community's encouragement of women to share their thoughts "explain" her as an author, why weren't there hundreds of her, and not just one? Of course, quantities of Montanist writings, perhaps including those of women, would have perished later under the hostile judgment of the strain of Christianity that would become dominant. But then why was *her* testimony (granted, as always, the removal of any statements that could not be massaged into orthodoxy) irresistible? How did it survive to be admired today?

It was not, evidently, supreme dedication to her religion—though she is shown dying for that religion—that made her a literary star. There were many other martyrs, many of whom suffered more, or more dramatically, and some of whom spoke or wrote in the first person. But none of the others gives so plausible an account of what it was like to be a person gifted with such a calling, who had to live through the time between the heady first inspiration and the final sacrifice of the self. Declaiming is not recognizable as living. Christian writers of proven commitment could be dull or bombastic about martyrdom as a general, lofty, cause—something in which the redactor shows a great interest and in which Perpetua shows almost none. She is instead preoccupied with her hardships, her family, her present role, and her extra share of glory in heaven.

But to call her narrow would be to miss the moral dimension of writing and speaking that so many male Roman writers dilated

Her Own Hand, Her Own Impressions

on, even as they flouted it themselves: style shows character. In *Flight in Time of Persecution*, Tertullian elaborately decries the option of leaving a city for safety; he even deconstructs Jesus's command to his disciples to do that very thing, not once but again and again.[6] Yet Tertullian is said to have died of old age, not in the arena or by beheading. Saturus, the instructor of Perpetua's group of martyrs, shows what can be done by doing it: he turns himself in. As I argued earlier, if the edict of Severus exempted from punishment anyone who was not proselytizing or proselytized, established Christians could get their share of holy vulnerability by preaching, teaching, or baptizing. Perpetua does not complain of generalship from far behind the lines in the fight against Satan, but her diary is a reproach in itself. She gives her life, and gives her account of the time before giving it; she does not tell other people what to do, filling the space for action with mere words, in the classic rhetorical manner.

The conventional flowery, hortatory, and impersonal style of Perpetua's redactor, especially in his preface, shows by contrast why her own work is so special. First him, then her, in a return to the passage we examined earlier in the discussion of her relationship with her father:

> Indeed, "In the last days," says the Master, "I will pour out my Spirit onto everyone alive, and their sons and daughters will speak out; and on my slaves, both men and women, I will pour out my Spirit; and the young men will see visions, and the old men will dream dreams."[7] Therefore even we — who recognize and honor both the original prophecies and the new visions that are pledged in parallel, and count the other powers of the Holy Spirit as instruction for the Church (to which that same Spirit was sent issuing largess to all the people, just as the Master shares it out to individuals) — have no choice but to both set out

such things and make them known through reading aloud for the glory of God, so that no one who is weak or despairing about his faith should think that divine grace was a companion only of the ancients, whether it was granted in the form of martyrs or of revelations; since God always accomplishes what he has promised as evidence for those who do not believe and as a favor to those who do.[8]

While we were still with our attendants, (she says), and my father wanted to turn my resolve upside down with his talk and wouldn't leave off trying to bring me down, because he felt so strongly for me, I said, "Father, do you see — just to give an example — that container lying there, a little pitcher or whatever it is?" And he told me, "Yes." And I told him, "It can't be called by any other name than what it is, can it?" And he said, "No." "It's the same way with me. I can't say that I'm anything other than what I am, a Christian." Then my father, reacting to this word, threw himself at me to tear my eyes out, but he only roughed me up, and he went away defeated, along with the arguments the devil had given him. For the next few days when I didn't have my father around, I thanked the Master, and it was heavenly for me that *he* was gone. In this actual interval of a few days, we were baptized.[9]

Conventional Latin writing defends its own existence word by word, and inserts itself into a long succession. A typical Latin author, such as the redactor, takes the focus off himself and refers to higher authority; for Christians, of course, it is God and the Bible: the redactor solidifies his argument with quotations.

The redactor's second sentence here is eighty-three words long in Latin. The opening of Milton's *Paradise Lost* is roughly comparable in its elaborative ambition. Yet the redactor is not displaying poetic virtuosity but adhering to an ordinary standard for formal communication in his time. Roman rhetoric is often "periodic," meaning literally that it takes "the road around." In modern editions and translations, a period marks the gasping pause after one of these odysseys of clauses, a grand tour of the point the writer is making, with all its explanations, qualifications, digressions, and other coloring.

But a little later the redactor begins to transcribe what he claims are Perpetua's own words, and the style of the prose alters resoundingly. Her first sentence, at section 3.1, is only twenty-eight words long in Latin, and it is broken up clearly and neatly. The redactor himself falls in with her stress on the plainspoken word, adding the verb *inqam*, or "say" (in my translation, "she says"), a common means of reporting dialogue in Latin, and perhaps a hint that she dictated her account instead of writing it out by herself as the redactor claims.[10] (But there are stronger reasons than this to doubt that she wrote by hand. What kind of time, space, and privacy could a jail afford to a young woman in the act of writing, and how securely could she have kept her tablets or her scroll in its bulky case?) She in fact quotes herself speaking to her father, using the same verb for "say." Then she switches to *dico* ("he told" and "I told" in my translation), another common verb for reporting speech, and then varies this with the even more colloquial *ait* (literally, "he says," my "he said") and uses another *dico* (in indirect speech, my "say that I'm") a little later.

The manner here is typical of Perpetua: short, active, colloquial sentences with the action on top and the reasoning more or less assumed, not interwoven as if for an audience unfamiliar with the background and themes of the story—which makes sense if this document was read aloud in Christian assemblies: the listeners knew what martyrdom was about. But given the early Christian penchant for copiously pious utterance (as evidenced by so many other texts that circulated), the starkness of this account is surprising. Perpetua's language is imbued with Vulgar Latin, literally the Latin of the common people, which moved toward the cultural center during the Roman imperial period. Bible translation in Latin was in this strain, but, again, Perpetua's account does not sound like the Bible in any language, with stilted repetitions and formulas; she sounds like a confident oral storyteller among friends. And she could hardly sound less like the typical church father. She does not, for example, reflect on the morality or the metaphysics or the cosmology of her father's trying to talk her out of martyrdom; he merely leaves "with the arguments the devil had given him." (Don't get Tertullian started on the role of the devil in thwarting martyrdom — or anything else good and necessary.) Throughout her portion of the *Suffering*, she will use specifically Christian language, when she does use it, in this way — as *expressive* language, arranging elements for her own purposes, linking old resonances together to make a new story.

For example, three instances of her praying punctuate her account of her dead brother Dinocrates' salvation. She starts by describing the whole group as simply "praying," an act that causes her to cry out his name. Then she realizes that she can pray for a vision of him, and this prayer is rendered in phrasing with a biblical flavor: "I began to say a prayer for him with great feeling, and to moan to God in sorrow." But her climactic prayer, the one that needs to be powerful enough to rescue the boy, shows in its description a biblical plenitude rare for her: "And I said prayers for him day and night, groaning and weeping to be given what I prayed for."[11] She thus employs stronger language of religious authority as she shows her own power prevailing.

In many other ways, she deploys literary elements with skill and confidence, though subtly and without pretension. The scene in which she confronts her father is a private prelude to the hearing before the procurator at which each of the Christian prisoners will say the fatal words, "I am a Christian." A connecting topos is physical attack: her roughing up at her father's hands and her father's beating at the hearing; for emphasis, she claims to have suffered, as if in her own body, what happened to him.[12] It might be argued that she is merely reporting things that happened and things she felt, but the extreme economy of her narrative makes her choices important and her parallels notable. The combination of selectivity and realism makes for a *meaningful* coherence. It is infused with an individual experience, but it communicates powerfully to other people, including those who have very little in common with her.

This effect goes some way toward explaining the special popularity of Perpetua's story in Late Antiquity — it spawned a conspicuous cult, which left many images of her — and the special interest Perpetua evokes now. Most martyrs are seen from far outside performing their testimony, and they perform it with implausible and dull perfection; they are too little like people and too much like props. Or if they are writing in the first person, they mainly preach. There is no vivid sense of what they went through, so the deeper religious message — of the hopelessness of humankind on its own, and of its mysterious transformation through God's love and power — is lost.

Even in details of style, Perpetua's storytelling works plausibly and artfully toward this message. Her colloquialisms, for example, sound genuine, but they are not sloppy; they are put to great effect. Classical Latin tends not to use subject pronouns except for emphasis (the differences between "I" "you" "we," "he," "she," "it," and "they" are embedded in the forms of the Latin verb, making these pronouns unnecessary for conveying the basic sense of an utterance), whereas in Vulgar Latin they creep in more and more and prefigure their indispensability in modern Romance languages. Such a blatant egotist as Julius Caesar saw no need for an explicit *ego*, "I," in his *veni, vidi, vici* (I came, I saw, I conquered) boast about the conquest of Gaul. Perpetua writes *ego* twice in reporting on her short interchange with her father, making it quite clear that *she* asked him whether it would be correct to misname the pitcher, and that *she* could not be called anything but a Christian.

Yet she does not just splash her ego (either the word or the sense of self) artlessly across the narrative. Here, her first *ego* is merely part of a speech attribution, "And I told him" in my translation. Consider oral narration in French, for example: *Moi, j'ai dit* ... (Me, I said ...). This is comfortably assertive, and it also serves to set speakers and actors apart more clearly. Perpetua's second *ego*, though, is key; it appears as the third Latin word in a sentence that reads in English, literally, "Thus also I am not able to call myself anything else but what I am, a Christian." The self — expressed here by two forms of the Latin word *ego, ego* and *me*, and by the "I" inherent in the verbs *possum* and *sum*, "I am able" and "I am" — clangs through her assertion. The *ego* alone is so emphatic that in my translation I render the single word as "It's the same way with me." But I hope that a matter-of-fact, even tone expresses that she is not boasting; she is asserting not her power but God's: God has transformed her whole self and placed it at his own disposal. As usual, though, the idea is not spelled out as an idea but expressed more effectively through what is believably happening: a feisty postadolescent has had a dangerous religious conversion and is facing off with her father about it, showing how absolute their rift needs to be, a rift that indicates how close they were before. This personal exchange helps place the depiction of transcendent gifts — worth any price — that follows in other scenes in a vivid light.

This use of *ego* is a small thing, but it suggests that aesthetics and literary purpose should weigh in our judgment of Perpetua's self-regard. Her self-glorification can be off-putting, but when the

Her Own Hand, Her Own Impressions

issue is her character as a woman *writer*, I am inclined to cut her a good deal of slack. Before the twentieth century (and well into it), a woman's world was narrow; we probably cannot imagine how narrow it was in the ancient world. From Sappho to Virginia Woolf, in any event, women authors had to work with what they had, and a ready source of fascination was the self; the psychological depths of the self for Perpetua, however, come into the brightest light in the visionary passages, which I am saving for my next chapter.

Another Vulgar Latin feature to consider is the use of the transitions *et* (and) and *tunc* (then) as sentence starters. These transitions do not need any explanation as part of colloquial storytelling, but they serve Perpetua especially handily. The words skip the reader from one scene to another with vague intervals and no causal links expressed; details are swallowed up in the forward movement, which has a natural, freewheeling feel. As the first narrative sequence continues, this mode takes Perpetua through some quite gapped and jagged territory. What kind of superior quarters did the bribe buy for the group? How did they come to be paroled, and why was it only for a time? Why was Perpetua's baby starving without her? Why did she have to make a special arrangement with her mother and brother for the child's care? How did she then come to have the child with her in prison, and for how long, and why only once? How and why was he taken from her?

The text here is geared toward news of providence, with the same kind of necessary whipsawing between prescribed Christian messaging and social realities as is evident elsewhere in the narrative. Later, Perpetua reports within two sentences that her father will not give the baby back to her, that the baby has weaned himself of his own accord, and that the pain in her breasts from residual milk has ceased.[13] She never shows herself letting his care or welfare get in the way of her mission; she is not even supposed to think about yielding to the pressure of her father and the magistrate for these (or any) reasons. Yet her appeal would certainly diminish if she were shown coldly allowing the child to suffer and fall into peril. Also, if she appeared subject to the ordinary consequences of what she does it would throw into doubt the idea of God's special favor toward her; her less friendly contemporaries could call it a punishment, for example, if her breasts were swollen or perhaps infected due to her intermittent nursing. Hence the reader is told that the pain stops, but never that it starts. She is such a good narrator, however, that these discrepancies do not surface on a first or even a second reading. At those stages I felt Perpetua naturally, sympathetically turning her attention to her child rather than her martyrdom; her manner is so ingenuous that I did not question her.

Perpetua also does not state why the group ended up in the stocks, only that they were there when the second vision of Dinocrates — his release from the proto-purgatory — came to her.[14] A narrative that balanced the prisoners' misery against the boy's salvation would throw the entire theme of the *Suffering* into doubt. Earthly woes must appear trivial, not worth mentioning except as a reminder that heaven cannot cost too much. In yet another instance of careful narrative engineering — though Perpetua is no longer speaking or writing at this point — Felicitas, who invites an excruciating premature birth in order not to lose her share in the coming execution spectacle, is not described as worrying about any danger to the baby, or, in fact, giving thought to the baby at all; she simply gives birth to a girl at the end of her ordeal. No word of regret or hesitation marks Felicitas's surrender of her baby; it is not even stated that she does surrender her (that would require one of the rather sinister Latin verbs of "giving up" or "handing over"), only that a Christian woman raises the baby as a daughter — that is, not as a slave. A doleful sign of Felicitas's loss registers only later, and

Her Own Hand, Her Own Impressions

only to the pagan audience, to enable them to pity the young woman, admire her fortitude, and tacitly admit the cruelty of the proceedings: the naked postpartum breasts are dripping milk.[15]

Perpetua does not come across as merely a storyteller making astute use of a plain-sounding style. As I noted, the colloquial register in Latin literature was, as a rule, self-consciously sexed up; Vulgar Latin itself could include stiff archaisms, obscure technical terms, and exotic-sounding foreign-derived words, all of which even a monumental poet like Vergil could deploy to great effect. Perpetua's outstanding trick is to add attention grabbers without any air of contrivance, as if unusual usages just came to her mind at times as the only way to express things. When she dismisses her father for what she clearly hopes is the last time, her "comfort" takes a didactic and queenly form: "What God wants will be done on that platform for the accused. Be cognizant that we do not exist under our own power, but that of God."[16] The Latin is even more pompous, with somewhat unusual word order and a rare future imperative (my "Be cognizant"). In the next episode, the magistrate condemns her to death, but she does not quote him doing so; this omission itself helps make her point: as God's favored agent, she is the real authority, the one whose specific words matter.

Outside her first-person narrative, there is some evidence that her expression could be conventionally sophisticated. Perhaps signs of this sophistication were not permitted to survive in her own voice; here I am thinking of modern religious leaders who would rather quote women, keeping the narrative control, than let them communicate for themselves. This scene comes from the redactor:

> When the tribune was imposing more stringent restrictions on the prisoners than usual, because the warnings of the most empty-headed people had caused him to fear that they would be extracted from the

prison by certain magical spells, Perpetua answered him to his face: "Why on earth don't you allow us to enjoy ourselves? We're the most distinguished criminals, we clearly belong to Caesar, and we're going to fight on his birthday. Wouldn't it be to your great credit if we're fatter when we're led out there?" The tribune shuddered and turned red; and after this he ordered them to be treated more humanely, and the result was that her brothers and other people had the opportunity of coming in and enjoying their company—now that even the adjutant who ran the prison was a believer.[17]

Here Perpetua speaks like a rhetorical adept, using a clever oxymoron ("most distinguished criminals") and a glib analogy to gladiators. (She and her companions are technically mere prisoners condemned to execution.) She sounds like someone who has been a spectator at the games, or at least knows their lore and can play on technical angles of the physical contests, as orators were wont to do. Gladiators were artificially plump, with a thick outer layer of fat from a starchy diet, for the same reason sumo wrestlers are artificially obese: to perform a sporting ritual so esoteric that an extraordinary body type is required. In the case of gladiators, the fight was supposed to be long, hard, and bloody, so a dramatic gush of blood from a shallow and not disabling cut into capillary-rich fat could be a helpful special effect. How many people knew that this *was* a special effect, and how many could craft a clever joke about it? The tribune, in any event, is shown to be impressed with the cogency of her argument, if not with its witty framing as well. Maybe this is because she speaks like a fearless and clever *man* of her era: with casual sarcasm and a clear enough implied threat that not cooperating would be a bad idea.

More of her brainy sass comes as she and her friends prepare to enter the arena. They are dressed in pagan religious outfits that

Her Own Hand, Her Own Impressions

were probably chosen for their striking colors and ironic overtones: these prisoners are, after all, going to die because of their defiance of the Roman state religion. Perpetua is having none of it, and she verbally reshapes the event once more, but now she does not suggest that the martyrs have simply the bodies of gladiators; they have, and deserve, the same professional rights:

> And when they had been led up to the gate and were being forced to put on costumes, the men to be dressed as priests of Saturn, and the women as consecrated devotees of Ceres, that noble woman fought back stalwartly clear to the end. She in fact said, "We come here of our own will, so that our liberty will not be crushed. That's the reason we have given over our lives: to avoid doing anything like this. This is the contract we have made with you." Injustice recognized justice; the tribune gave in. Just as they were, in their ordinary clothes, they were led in.[18]

Perpetua adventurously overstates the case. Yes, a gladiator's fighting role and thus his costume could be fixed by contract, but talk of his *libertas,* his precious civic freedom (if he had had any in the first place) would have been a non sequitur: he was *addictus,* or given over like a slave; he might fight his way to moneyed retirement but not out of his social and political disabilities. Moreover, gladiators were a notoriously crude and degraded lot; it is extraordinary that a well-brought-up young woman is standing, even metaphorically, on her rights as a gladiator. This might be black humor, rather like a modern prisoner subjected to strip searches demanding fair pay as a prostitute.

But it is shown that Perpetua's argument wins: she obtains "justice," as if from her integrity and eloquence in court. Hers is a hugely more sophisticated sally than Saturus's charmless threats to the gawkers at the banquet the condemned are granted: "Tomorrow isn't enough for you? Why are you glad to see what you hate? Today you're friends, tomorrow you're enemies. But take a good look and remember our faces, so that you recognize us on that all-important day [of judgment]."[19]

In case I seem to be overstating Perpetua's success as a writer and speaker, I can compare the performance of her teacher Saturus, the other writer in the *Suffering* who plainly had not had a standard elite education, and also the other narrator who recounts a dream of heaven.[20] Perpetua's swiftness, clarity, punch, and originality may not seem like significant achievements until viewed side by side with the kind of mistakes nearly all of us commit in beginning composition class or as young creative writers who should read more before we write.

Saturus is fussy yet confusing. It would not matter which lore of the journey to heaven he is drawing on—there is plenty, both Christian and pagan—if he had not tied himself up in distracting knots. He writes that he and Perpetua are carried to heaven once they are dead, but he nervously adds that the four angels who lift them do not actually touch them.[21] This would be impossible anyway in the case of those who have left their physical bodies, so does the reader need it pointed out? If Saturus has edited the dream for metaphysical consistency, as a teacher might, that consistency falls away later, when Christ strokes the two martyrs' faces as they kiss him, and when the two exchange the kiss of peace.[22]

To return to the journey to heaven: Saturus carefully denies that the newly immortal pair are lying on their backs facing upward (like corpses), but he is unclear what position they are in. If they are (literally) "like those climbing a gentle slope," are they upright and walking, and if so, how and why are they being carried? The images and the narrative sequence of Perpetua's dreams may be choppy and in places inconsequential, but we can at least see what is happening.

Saturus's account presents more problems to textual critics and translators than does any passage Perpetua wrote. His description of the simple act of crossing a garden, walking a certain distance, or walking to another part of heaven is awkward and unclear, and a scribe may have made it worse by trying to clarify it.[23] Saturus also has himself and Perpetua asking (literally) "them where they were" or "them where the rest were"; in either case there is rudimentary failure in pronoun reference. Who is being asked about whom?[24] By this time, a number of angels have manifested in different ranks and capacities, plus three martyrs whom Saturus and Perpetua recognize on meeting them; an array of other immortals and two mortals will appear later.

Speaking of angels, Saturus's repetitions about them sound like a child's excited prattle. "There in the garden were four other angels, shining brighter than the rest. And when they saw us, they greeted us in terms of honor, and they said with great awe to the rest of the angels, 'Here they are — here they are!' and the four angels who were carrying us were filled with awe, and put us down."[25] He uses for a building or other enclosure the Latin word that usually means a mere place, which is hardly fatal, but harping on such a simple word sounds very unsophisticated. "And we came up to a place, and the walls around this place seemed to be built out of light, and in front of the gate of that place four angels were standing who dressed us in shining white robes as we went in."[26] The repetitions may be biblical in manner, but to the educated Roman ear, the Latin Bible sounded very crude; it did not offer a style to imitate.

Overall, Saturus is extremely diffuse, perhaps influenced by previous lingering imagery of heaven, as in the *Apocalypse of Peter*.

Perpetua

Perpetua in her vision of heaven notes nothing of the landscape but an immense garden and nothing animated in it but sheep, a white-clad crowd, and a shepherd figure: she is riveted on the shepherd Christ, and they come together like two magnets. Saturus presents us with an entire heavenly bureaucracy, and his heavenly scenery is a baffling mish-mash, with flowering trees as big as cypresses, and continually falling petals. What season is it, or are two seasons happening at once? He writes not that the trees were as tall as cypresses, but literally, "The loftiness of the trees was in the manner of cypresses."[27] I feel like treating the style the way Mark Twain treats that of James Fenimore Cooper and hacking such an overgrown sentence down to size.

After Saturus's dream narration, however, the return to the sententious redactor (or the redactor's handling of someone else's account of events running up to the games, and of the spectacle itself) makes me miss the relatively clean writing of Perpetua and Saturus both.

I noted earlier that Perpetua's writing reminds me of Anne Frank's. I see that resemblance first of all in its freshness and exuberant confidence. Called Mrs. Quack Quack by her teacher for talking too much, Frank wrote a story about Mrs. Quackenbush the duck, who with her voice alone defends her ducklings against a vicious black swan. As Perpetua writes fearlessly about nursing, mastitis, and weaning while in and out of prison, Anne Frank writes fearlessly about a toilet and bathing facilities shared by eight people who cannot make their presence known, and about sneaking off to an unused space to make out with the son of the other family in their hiding place.

But it is not self-revelation that makes these writers great; a flasher in a park reveals himself. Both their works share elements with women's literature at its best, when it counters human helplessness by means of women's irrepressible voices. Perpetua and Anne Frank were literally confined and at the mercy of immense forces during a contest for the future of the world. But they did not reach toward what they could have dealt with only incompetently — theology and martyrology in the one case, politics and war in the other. They faced matters close at hand, and within themselves, and made these into living arguments, arguments that leap off the page, for reverence for the human mind and spirit in whatever body it appears. I have prodded here and there at Perpetua's prose in an effort to explain exactly how she did it, how an infected breast is packed with meaning, but literary effect is to some degree a mystery. Dr. Johnson's nasty pronouncement comes to mind, in which he compares a dog walking on its hind legs to a woman preaching and notes that "you are surprized to find it done at all." Surprise, curiosity, prurience may be first impressions, but they are not the means by which a story sticks; and certain women's stories stick like nothing else.

Perpetua's writing is sometimes treated condescendingly, as if her words pour childishly onto the page because of her narrow experience. But if an author pushes against a narrow personal framework, she may achieve something extraordinary. I think of Jane Austen's "3 or 4 families in a Country Village," through whose interactions she meditates on dignity and destiny; of Saint Thérèse of Lisieux's *Story of a Soul* with its "little way" to achieve a relationship with God; and of Anne Frank's diary. What makes certain women's writing literature in spite of everything is the superhuman-looking commitment not only to being oneself (any sociopath has that), and not only to becoming more than oneself and part of something much bigger; but also a commitment to sharing the imperfect and sometimes even shameful process — not always insightfully, not always honestly, but in one's own unforgettable words.

CHAPTER FOUR

I Knew I Spoke with the Master

Ironically, Perpetua's visions are the most coherent, roundly convincing parts of her narrative. This is not, of course, to call them logical or realistic. But unlike her account of her waking life, her visions show no glaring signs of editing, by her or anyone else. They evince the kind of emotion, plasticity, and vividness typical of ordinary dreams, as well as the supercharging with meaning that makes religious dreams speak to particular existential crises. If in the whole of her story she is unusually self-expressive, even using tropes of Christianity as a personal language, in her dreaming she can be almost defiant. There may be plenty that she experienced in sleep or in another visionary state that she does not choose to pass along—nightmares and ambiguous portents, for instance. But what she does pass along offers a touching sense of an inner life she would have had to erase in ordinary writing and conversation in order not to violate the conventions of martyrdom too outrageously. Among the things that, if they were not couched as involuntary revelations, would have endangered her standing among the living and in posterity are signs of her robust ego, of her deeper and more individual traumas, and of her changing and new relationships.

Perhaps the most disturbing aspect to a modern reader is the sense of her dreams as a practical contrivance, but here I think our own anachronistic judgment is to blame. Her community sought dreams from her because it was customary to seek them. Dreams and portents filled both ordinary and momentous needs and obligations in her pagan as well as her Christian culture, and dreams therefore fell under various auspices of transaction. Her "brother" (either biological or spiritual, but probably biological, as she uses the optional possessive pronoun in her Latin phrasing, thereby emphasizing the relationship) flatteringly nudges her into her first recorded dream.[1] She instantly and confidently, if also in reverent language, promises him results overnight. The role of the divinity in this compact is limited to a rather impersonal and colorless few words: the great favors the master has done her so far have convinced her that she can speak with him; but her interchange with heavenly power at this point, at least as revealed, is limited to praying and being shown the vision.

Visions were not usually a surprise visitation, like Jacob's ladder in Genesis 28, whose imagery is the basis for Perpetua's dream here; and even unexpected visions tended to address material crises like Jacob's exile. Willfulness rewarded was the norm. Biblical prophets might go out into the wilderness or (in Hebrew) the "place of speaking" to communicate with a divinity they were confident was there. Jesus in the Gospels leads his favorite followers up a mountain, where they see him transfigured and talking with Moses and Elijah, while Peter suggests building shelters for all three. The vision is sought out and understood at least in part as a transaction, as when pagans slept overnight in a temple and paid the god for the informative dreams they had there, or subcontracted the visioning by, for instance, paying for a priestess's drug-induced outpourings at the Delphi shrine. A pure, direct gift of a mystical message, such as Paul claims to have received in the "third heaven," was not only an exception: it was not, as a rule, of much use to the community. Paul lets his readers know that the actual content of his revelation is irrelevant to the matter at hand now, and indicates that such a lofty gift is a spiritual hazard.[2]

In line with the practical culture of envisioning, then, the brother who asks Perpetua for a dream wants to know whether the whole imprisoned group will be reprieved: he uses the word *commeatus*, "furlough," an earthy term conveying the typical warfare imagery of martyrdom. She closes her account of the detailed, personal-sounding, dramatic dream as if the experience had no purpose but to nerve them all for their trials: "And I immediately gave an account to my brother, and we understood that suffering was to come, and from then on we had no hope for anything in this world."[3]

Granted, the parties in the *Suffering* take disquietingly ad hoc and willful action — even for their time — in summoning dreams, especially this one. The ancients set aside certain places, times, cult practices, and guiding authorities for channeling the divine will through the receptive mind, and this sense of conventionality around dreaming does not appear to have changed substantially with Christianity. Granted, the New Prophecy movement may have offered forums that were unusually open for the post-apostolic era. The *Suffering*, if informed by that movement, would be the only direct and sympathetic source for what the resulting revelations sounded like. But as with all of Perpetua's writing, her accounts of her dreams seem to tell us a great deal about one extraordinary individual in her social world, and little that is new or interesting about any strain of religion.

As to some basic structures, the first dream is not the only one

Perpetua

with rather tritely pious words framing it, making her appear to be reciting what she is supposed to feel and how she is supposed to interpret. I am not surprised that a young, sheltered, naive, and self-involved woman leaned, even where her dreams were concerned, for direction on people she particularly trusted now that she has lost her home and everything reliable from her past. With a convert's zeal, she handed to those who had assumed authority over this episode of martyrdom whatever of her inner life she thought would be of use — but in between these handovers, she is bursting with images and narratives that cast her as the ancient version of a movie superhero, someone who has a transforming otherworldly encounter and rises to a new tier of power. The contrast between the meek, conventional Christian Perpetua and the vibrant Perpetua who is making of Christianity what she wants and needs it to be is even greater when it comes to the scenes within her mind. These appear like large, unique, bright, many-faceted though glaringly flawed jewels set in battered tin. I will go through the dreams in order to show what they suggest about the dreamer.

Her guide within the first vision, Saturus, is a very special person, the only Christian functionary who has volunteered to share the martyrs' imprisonment and death.[4] He is the only fellow martyr she herself ever mentions by name, and he was the group's teacher on the outside, presumably the man preparing them all for baptism; like the converts, he would have fallen under Severus's edict to prevent the spread of the religion (if that is in fact what the edict said); but Perpetua clearly thinks he could have escaped had he wanted to. And he, not she, receives the longest, concluding vision shown in the *Suffering*.[5]

Jacob's dream in Genesis 28 gives Perpetua a starting point for images and words, but she has very little there to go on. The only unique images in the Bible episode come in verse 12: the ladder or stairway to the sky with angels ascending and descending and God standing at the top. Perpetua's version is a baroque, very personal development of this scene. Her ladder is bronze, marvelously long, reaching "all the way" to the sky, and also narrow: only one person at a time can go up – there is apparently no safe way to climb down. Large, dangerous objects (most of them weapons) line the ladder, and she gives a short inventory, as well as a picture of the consequences of a single careless move: human gore on the metal, the gore's owners gone – fallen into hell, or back into a sinful life, or just disappearing in the illogical manner of dreams?

Maybe a real-life scene that has taken place already, or is feared, contributes to the dream. Martyrs reportedly were often tortured, and if this group was not, there may have been a threat of torture to reckon with, and possibly a tour of the instruments to make the threat immediate and credible. (The history of institutional torture in the West indicates that at some point this tour became more or less part of the protocol.) If Perpetua was exempt from torture through citizenship, gentility, or connections, her companions were not; and whatever her legal rights, her father went to great lengths in his efforts, perhaps in collusion with authorities, to make her recant. She could have had in mind agony and damage to her body not only in the arena but also outside it.

In part, her first vision is a mutilation dream founded on guilt or terror, but it includes elements of the climbing or flying dream of transcendence, and has a little of the late-arrival dream, a more extensive example of which is the beginning of Perpetua's vision in section 10: her journey to the arena is rough, winding, and exhausting, and she barely makes it. In the ladder dream, Saturus climbs up before Perpetua and calls down to her, but his words overcome any hint of rivalry or anxiety: he says he is waiting for her and warns her of the amazingly large snake, liable to bite her, lying under the ladder. Her climb, it transpires, is joyful from the start, and she climbs all the way up untroubled by the snake or any of the sharp gear: it was only before she began, and was staring at the combined hazards, that she was frightened.

This snake is a complex symbol. According to the lore of martyrdom he is the embodiment of fear, pain, and rationalization, the devil blocking the way to glory. He is also the snake in Eden responsible for the fall of humankind into sin. Part of God's punishing curse pronounced on the snake is, "I will put enmity between you and the woman, and between your offspring and her offspring; he will crush your head, and you will strike his heel."[6] Perpetua makes no reference to the misogyny in the original passage (the biblical curse turns more specifically to womankind in the next verse, with a decree of agonizing childbirth and submission to man), or of the extra misogyny heaped on by early Christian thinkers, who made woman herself the gateway to hell. Perpetua takes the male role in stamping on the snake's head, and the snake evinces no resistance. Just the opposite: he slowly, fearfully offers his head as a step; he is no match for her trust in Jesus to protect her from his fangs. But the keys to her safe and expeditious climb appear to be Saturus's encouragement and warning.

She reaches the top with supernatural ease (one word covers the long and scary-looking way through the sharp objects: *ascendi*, "I . . . climbed up") and finds a paradise on the same scale as the ladder: the garden is huge, and the shepherd is in the middle of it, tall or large. He is milking sheep, and many thousands of white-clad figures look on. The shepherd greets her, calling her "child" in Greek, calls her over to him, and gives her a piece of fresh curd from his milking: she takes it in her hands and eats it and can still taste its sweetness when she awakens.

A frequent pictorial image in very early Christian art is Jesus the

Good Shepherd, posed not in realistic rough and uninviting terrain (as a rule, sheep and goats did not graze on land where crops could have grown) but in some choice part of pastoral pleasure grounds such as the pagan idealizations of the countryside seen in conventional artwork. *The Apocalypse of Peter* describes a flourishing and ornamental heavenly landscape, and the title of *The Shepherd of Hermas* refers to a heavenly shepherd who is a guiding character. But neither these works nor the scriptures (except for the motif of banqueting, and that was kept quite general) nor the church fathers show a fully interactive, personally satisfying, sensuous experience of being in heaven. Perpetua was convinced that she could effectively keep and enjoy her own body, and that it would be like a well-cared-for child's.

Jesus of the Gospels is a young man; in early Christian iconography he tends to be a beardless, pretty, Dionysus- or Apollo-like figure. (The book of Revelation gives him white hair.)[7] But Perpetua does not subscribe to the prevailing imagery. For her, Jesus, with his tender address as to a daughter and his gift of sweet curd (like the ritual drink celebrating baptism), is a venerable, all-powerful nurturer and encourager to replace her earthly father, whose love turned into a panicked drive for control. The white-robed throngs who stand around say, "Amen," the way they seal their chants of praise to the enthroned Lamb himself in Revelation. Saturus has faded out after his arrival; he does not greet Perpetua when she arrives after him, and no one appears to notice him.

Her second vision, in section 7, is not at anyone's prompting. How could it be? She notes that her brother Dinocrates' terrible death during childhood "never" occurred to her except on this occasion, when in the middle of the group's prayers his name burst out of her. She must mean that she has not thought of him since the events of her martyrdom began; his death from a facial lesion (probably cancer or an infection) must have impressed her viscerally at the time, and she would not have forgotten him as soon as he was buried.

The episode of this even more intimate dream starts in the text immediately after her father refuses to give her her baby back and she has closed the book on motherhood. Now that she is condemned and in prison again, she does not mention her mother, and her brother the convert is mentioned only one more time, in the account of the games: he is brought to her when she is at the Gate of Life, apparently being offered a reprieve (which is plainly not regarded as an option).[8] The father she rejects does visit her again later, but only with more pleas to recant, which she scorns.[9] She is cut off from her family, with the prospect of an immediate path to heaven but no prospect of sharing it soon with anyone from the home she grew up in or married into.

She faces this emptiness with spiritual and emotional resourcefulness. She sees her long-dead brother, in miserable squalor and thirst, across a huge gulf (that naive or melodramatic-sounding emphasis on size again; she sounds to me almost like a child using the American English word, "big-giant"): they cannot reach each other. Her situation is like that of the kind widow who hosts Thecla before her appearance in the arena in the pious novel: her daughter has died unbaptized and so cannot go to heaven: she needs a truly heroic intervention, which the magically holy, brave, and invulnerable Thecla provides. Perpetua provides such an intervention for her own relative. Dinocrates first appears in a proto-purgatory, where the unbaptized dead languish. But the others remain in the shadowy background: only the boy emerges, parched but unable to reach the rim of a pool filled with water. She narrates how she, once awake, makes use of her privileged status with God and prays with intense though stereotypical passion for the boy in his suffering.

I Knew I Spoke with the Master

She never shows herself as exercised as at this point: "And I said prayers for him day and night, groaning and weeping to be given what I prayed for."[10]

In her own dismal confinement in the stocks some days later, she sees her dead brother clean, well dressed, healed of his lesion, and drinking as much as he likes, ceaselessly drawing over the lowered rim of the pool what must be the pure, eternally abundant water of baptism. In a highly Perpetuan manner, she combines the holy and ineffable with the mundane, feminine, and emotional. Like herself as a little girl or teenager looking after a younger brother, and like a mother caring for her baby, she is heartsick until he is healthy and clean and nicely dressed and has a drink; and she takes no thought for other people's competing needs. In her eyes, the boy shows the same distinction from the crowd of hopeless souls who remain in the dark as he would have shown while alive from the household slaves: he is the one whose feelings and fate matter. He is also at first like her in jail, conspicuously fallen from his former comforts. As a young lady, she was used to regular baths and changes of clothes, clean bedding, comfortable furniture, and pleasant, enclosed outdoor places, their air freshened by evaporating water. In a religious sense, the boy obtains his first baptism, and she is awaiting her proverbial second, martyrdom's baptism by blood. Like his, her ritual is destined to be special, in a bright foreground.

I have not seen any evidence of women in the early church holding authority over baptism; Perpetua had only recently been baptized herself, and is certainly not mature or learned enough to instruct others in preparation. But she assumes a breathtaking power with a breathtaking speed and naturalness. The setting is a homey but respectable one, a courtyard with a cistern from which the household drinks, but which a very small child could not reach into if it is built above the surface of the ground instead of dug into it.

Perpetua

In a typical Perpetuan over-the-top (sorry) touch, he drinks from a gold drinking bowl that never empties, leaving the reader to ask why he needs to keep drawing water — but dreams lack such practical cohesion: things in them just happen.

Then (as I read the Latin; it is not completely clear) Dinocrates gets into the pool and begins to splash around like a typical boy. Not only does Perpetua rescue a beloved family member through these two dreams; she dilates on her conception of heaven as a renewal of life as a beloved and carefree child. She and those she loves are not going to do any chanting of eternal praises; they will be able to return to what they most enjoyed in the past. A word for "relax" or "find relief" or "enjoy oneself" (states that are associated with salvation) occurs several times in her writing, and it is nearly always mistranslated; it literally means "cool down": the Latin is *refrigero*. This would have been a particularly resonant metaphor in North African Carthage, where the mother of all pleasures was to beat the heat in Roman-style amenities. "Cool down" does suggest children splashing in a garden on a hot day or friends enjoying a plunge pool together in the public baths.

Perpetua's fourth vision, in section 10, occurs the day before the games. She designates the vision by the Greek word *horoma*, which is a slightly different spelling of a word that occurs occasionally in the New Testament (though not in Revelation). (To catch the oddity, I have rendered it as "this seeing" in my translation.)[11] She dreams that the Christian assistant (or deacon) Pomponius has come and is knocking violently at the prison door. He has been an important link between the jailed Perpetua and the outside world: he gave a bribe to improve conditions for all the martyrs, and he acted as a messenger to her father, asking for her to have custody of the baby.[12] It would logically have been Pomponius who broke the news to her that she could not have her child back. Now Pomponius appears

I Knew I Spoke with the Master

on his own to lead only her to the amphitheater; it is as if her companions have disappeared and the ordeal and the glory will be hers alone.

> The day before we were to fight, I saw this seeing: Pomponius the minister had come to the gate of the prison and was knocking violently. And I came out to him and opened up to him. He was dressed in a white garment without a belt, and footwear with complicated laces. And he said to me, "Perpetua, we're waiting for you: come." And he held my hand, and we started to walk by rough, winding paths. It took a long time, and we barely made it, gasping for breath, to the amphitheater. He took me to the middle of the arena, and said to me, "Don't be frightened. I'll be here with you, struggling along with you." Then he went away.
>
> Then I saw a huge crowd, extremely excited. But since I knew that I was condemned to face wild animals, I was surprised that no animals were sent against me. Instead, an Egyptian, hideous in his appearance, came out along with his helpers to fight with me. But handsome young men came up to me, my own helpers and supporters. I was stripped down and became like a man. And my crew started to rub me down with oil, the way they usually do for an athletic contest. And opposite me I saw the Egyptian rolling in the wrestling sand. And there came out a man of an amazing size, so that he was actually taller than the highest point of the amphitheater. He was dressed without a belt, in purple, with two stripes over the middle of his chest, and in the same kind of footwear, intricately made of gold and silver, and he was carrying a switch, as if he were a trainer of gladiators, and a green branch that had gold apples on it. And he called for silence and said, "This Egyptian, if he defeats her, will kill her with a sword. But if she defeats him, she will receive this branch." Then he withdrew, and the two of us approached each other and started to throw punches. He was

trying to catch hold of my feet, but I was kicking him hard in the face. Then I was lifted up into the air and started to kick him so that it seemed I didn't step on the ground at all. But when I saw there was a pause in the action, I put my hands together, interlocked my fingers, and grabbed his head. And he fell face down, and I stamped on his head. Then the crowd started to shout, and my supporters started to sing a holy song, and I went up to the trainer and took the branch. And he kissed me and said to me, "Daughter, peace be with you." And I started to walk in glory toward the Gate of Life, and then I woke up. And I understood that I wasn't going to fight the wild animals but the devil; I knew, however, that I would have the victory.

To offset my initial judgment of solipsistic showboating here, I bear in mind that this narrative is in line with the nature of dreams. Even if a dream is about an erotic encounter, it will probably be more self-centered than waking sex, and the dreamed partner more instrumental to physical release. The now unfashionable Freud was certainly right about the expression of repressed desires through dreams (though the desires they express cannot all be fundamentally erotic, as he claimed), and Perpetua has already made it clear that she wants more care and attention than she can get even as the star of a group of martyrs facing execution.

As to the loud knocking, she might have incorporated into the dream some noise in the jail that did not completely wake her up. The term "the day before" (and not "the night before") that opens her account may indicate that she was taking a nap — the ordinary Roman afternoon nap she was used to, or perhaps a sleep of exhaustion or escape. But the image of knocking at a door occurs a number of times in the New Testament, and it stands for a calling to holiness. A passage in Revelation may in particular have helped inform this dream. Jesus has a message for one of his churches:

I Knew I Spoke with the Master

> I advise you to buy from me gold refined by fire so that you may become rich, white garments so that you may be clothed and your shameful nakedness not exposed, and salve to anoint your eyes so that you may see. Those I love, I rebuke and discipline. Therefore take me seriously and show remorse.
>
> Look, I am standing at the door and knocking. If anyone hears my voice and opens the door, I will come in and have dinner with him, and he with me. To the one who is victorious, I will grant the right to sit with me on my throne, just as I overcame and sat down with my father on his throne.[13]

In Perpetua's vision, note the precious gold prize to be won, Pomponius's white robe like a martyr's, the stripping to nakedness and anointing, the stress on divinely assisted vision, and the single victor over the forces of evil. In Saturus's dream, moreover, is an accessible divine throne: angels lift Saturus and Perpetua onto or above the lap of the throned Christ, where they kiss him and he strokes their faces.[14] The passage from Revelation is packed with parallels to dream imagery in the *Suffering;* but as usual the passage is not quoted, as a church father would quote it, but interwoven in a personal narrative.

It is hard, however, to account for one detail in the dream, Pomponius's and the referee's unusual footwear. Commentators disagree as to where it falls on the spectrum ranging from a soldier's boots to embroidered slippers. The word for the footwear is the first attestation of the Latin *galliculae,* and this may be a new or local word. The shoes might reflect the elaborate costumes worn by performers at the games. Alternately, the image (whatever it is) might simply represent the kind of odd, extraneous-seeming detail that dreams are prone to. Freud argues cogently that dreams contain memories lost to the conscious mind. Perpetua was raised to wear clothes worthy of her status, and if they are not on her list of concerns now, they still have emotional meaning for her: they represent care, indulgence, security. Early Christian authorities condemn finery—her compatriot and contemporary Tertullian does so quite vociferously—but that does not mean that she rejects the very notion of it or bars reminiscences of it from her spiritual world.

This dream at first breathes anxiety about lateness, which stands for a more general failure or inadequacy; the modern equivalent would be a dream about the struggle to reach a life-changing exam on time. Her guide tells her, "Perpetua, we're waiting for you: come"—the same kind of message that Saturus sends down the ladder to her before she starts to climb—and the two have a hard journey to the amphitheater. Real physical exhaustion and stress from the weeks in prison may register here, as both Perpetua and Pomponius are "gasping for breath" when they arrive at the amphitheater. As a possible literary influence, in *The Shepherd of Hermas*, a spiritual guide leads the narrator on a rough and pathless journey through the mountains as a preliminary to a vision.[15]

There is more than one way to read, in contrast to his immediate departure, Pomponius's Christlike command to Perpetua not to fear, as he will stay and struggle with her. Long passages of the Gospel of John are dedicated to Jesus's explanation at the Last Supper of his ongoing presence and return, despite his going away. But as a bald matter of what *happens* as depicted in the *Suffering*, Pomponius's promise and departure in the dream look rather odd. He reminds me a little of Perpetua's fellow Carthaginian and contemporary Tertullian's insisting to martyrs that they joyfully endure the full ordeal, while no part of it is going to touch his own body.

Pomponius leaves Perpetua to participate in a superstar athletes' contest. The crowd is huge (size again!). Because she knew that she was condemned to face wild animals, she is surprised not to see any. Instead, her hideous Egyptian opponent—again, a characteristic stress on the visual—comes out with his helpers. I am not going to wade far out into the ink spilled concerning his ethnicity; the suggestion may come from an actual contest Perpetua had seen, or from the fame of Egyptians for wrestling. Sodom and Egypt are associated with the beast in Revelation, and a specifically Christian racism extended beyond Jews to include other non-Europeans; Tertullian himself propagated it.[16] But though these would be plausible enough reasons for an Egyptian to embody the devil who wars against a martyr's faith, the text itself, as usual, seems to go to the heart of the matter: this is an *ugly* Egyptian.

Though mainstream Greek and Roman racism did take into account the troublesomeness of conquered and subordinate people, so that whole nations were labeled as wicked or uncivilized (the reputation of indigenous Egyptians did not evolve happily during the earliest centuries of European imperialism), the shorthand stigma might rest on looks: the wrong lips, hair, beards, even legs. Christians scorned the flesh, but Perpetua is only a recent convert, and as a young matrona she must have devoted time to her appearance before she went out in public, received guests, or even faced her own slaves, from whom she needed to maintain the proper visual distinctions. This would be only part of the enculturation that has left her with a deeply rooted judgment: the *bad* and *threatening* are *ugly*. In contrast, her own entourage is made up of *handsome* young men.

They strip her down and rub her with oil, the usual preparations for wrestling; hence I do not think that anything deeply meaningful, much less a modern type of gender transformation, lies in her turning literally "masculine" at this point, but only a dream's adjustment (during or after the dreaming) away from something untenable. The alternative image would be a young lady's body appearing voluntarily naked in this most public setting, and young male hands all over it, and then that body clashing with the body of a hideous foreigner, who presumably is naked too.

By subtracting breasts and adding a penis, the vision, or the memory of it, or its narration, protects her modesty while letting her engage in the ultimate masculine sport, a sport that was especially popular in North Africa. There were women gladiators in the Roman world, and women who fenced for private exercise; respectable women might swim and play certain athletic games with each other. But I have not heard of a woman wrestler before the modern era. Certainly, however, Perpetua's dream role as a male wrestler would not be degrading in comparison with a gladiator fight ("filthy gladiator" or "gladiator pervert" was a popular insult, and some elite Romans liked deploring the brutality of the combats they watched with fascination), and most especially not in comparison with her real upcoming experience of a prolonged execution in the arena. In fact, with her new body, her minder and escort Pomponius, and her sporty entourage preparing her for what will be a bloodless contest (though the category of no-holds-barred pankration wrestling, which this seems to be, was a rough and dangerous one), she could be making a bid through her dream to the status she has lost in society and more, as if she were a well-brought-up Greek boy trained in the gymnasium and fit to appear at international athletic competitions like the Olympics. These were in decline in Late Antiquity, but, unlike Roman gladiator games, they stood for the unsullied quest for individual glory through physical prowess.

Perpetua has the upper hand before the contest begins. While her entourage rubs her down, her opponent only rolls in the sand, like an animal. To apply a layer of sand on top of the oil was usual, but in her case we hear nothing about this gritty ritual. Familiarly,

I Knew I Spoke with the Master

Perpetua's notions become super-exuberant in the freedom of sleep, verging toward extremes and into the lushly visual. The figure who now arrives is taller than the stadium, and his flowing robe is not white but costly purple and striped like a magistrate's. His shoes (again, *galliculae*) are not only decorated with elaborate designs but made of silver and gold. He has a rod like the official at athletic games who is empowered to punish fouls, but also a green branch with golden apples on it. This might be a combination of the palm branch of victory and of eternal life, of both pagan and Christian significance; and the golden apples are at home in Greek mythology and literature. The man who carries the branch is a referee, a master of ceremonies, and a glitzy Christ at the same time; as usual in the *Suffering* dreams, he gives the impression of being a mature man.

It is not to be an open, fair competition for the precious branch. The giant announces skewed terms: the Egyptian, if victorious, gets to kill her with a sword, but if she wins (in martyrdom's real terms, that means bravely submitting to death), she will have the prize — it is not for the Egyptian, whatever the outcome. This is, in other words, a contest she can lose only if she foolishly chooses to trade a glorious eternal life for temporary physical survival. The actual fight is skewed as well: the Egyptian has no chance of winning because she can fly (another image of rising, as in the ladder dream), levitating above the range of his punches and kicking at will; she even steps on his head, as she stepped on the head of the snake in the first dream. (This also feels like a woman's mental adjustment to her lack of the upper-body strength that would give her any hope against a male wrestler face-to-face.) As the crowd shouts and her entourage sings a hymn, she goes to claim her prize from the official, who now greets her as "daughter" and gives her the Christian kiss of peace; he would never have allowed her to lose. She proceeds "in glory" toward the Gate of Life — ordinarily off-limits to convicts. When she awakens, she realizes that she is about to fight the devil and win, instead of fighting the beasts. She might have cribbed this conclusion from Tertullian; it is one of her commonplaces that set their context off as extraordinary.

Saturus's vision in sections 11–13 of the *Suffering* is worth consideration in tandem with Perpetua's visions; it is so similar that I believe she influenced it. At one point the male martyrs confer over their plans for the most personally suitable and satisfying deaths in the arena, as if they were planning a performance or strategizing in a sport.[17] If they did not consider such preparations frivolous or offensive, then why could Saturus and Perpetua not unselfconsciously have collaborated on their dreams, given that they were so close and so full of admiration for one another? I even wonder whether this might be her own final vision, ascribed to him; it comes close to the end of the story, when the men are shown taking on larger roles and the women fall back relative to them. (The men snarl at the gawkers during the ritual feast and provoke the spectators and the governor with their taunts.[18] They also go through lengthier and more harrowing trials in the arena.)

As in Perpetua's first vision, in Saturus's climactic one the two martyrs rise to heaven together. Now they are side by side, supported but untouched by four angels. An endless light appears ahead of them, and Saturus tells Perpetua that they have attained what they were promised.

Once again, providence is a personal, exclusive provision. The large garden-like space does not come into view, and they do not arrive at it: it is literally "made for us" (my translation is "opened up in front of us") as the angels carry the pair. The rose trees are as high as cypresses, the tallest trees in the hemisphere, and the petals fall continuously, filling the air with beauty. As for the angels already there, "when they saw us, they greeted us in terms of honor, and they said with great awe to the rest of the angels, 'Here they are – here they are!' and the four angels who were carrying us were filled with awe, and put us down." Meeting three other martyrs who have died in the same persecution but at different times and by different means, Saturus and Perpetua ask where the rest are (if that is what the text means; it is unclear here), but the angels tell them to first come and greet the Master.[19]

The Master is another unusual Christ, white-haired but with a youthful face. He is surrounded by elders. But the chanting in Greek of "Holy, holy, holy," as in Revelation, will not be any business of the newcomers; this deity is not welcoming them into any such role, or into any fixed role at all. They stand awestruck before the throne, but then angels lift them effectively into the Master's lap, where they can kiss him and he can stroke their faces, and after they ritually stand and exchange the kiss of peace (only with each other, or with the elders too?), the elders tell them, "Go and play." Like a father or elder brother, Saturus tells Perpetua, "You have what you want," and she assures him that she is even happier than before.[20]

They are waylaid, however, by two projections from mortal life, a bishop and an "elder" (a word that would be used later in history to designate a priest), who are quarreling on earth. They throw themselves at the new arrivals' feet and beg to be reconciled. Perpetua reproaches them, "our papa, and you an elder," for behaving this way. She does not want a replay of her father's high-pressure behavior, and in this scenario the foisting of responsibility on her is indeed ridiculous. But Perpetua and Saturus do graciously embrace those they have left behind, and are beginning a conference with them in a secluded part of the garden (Perpetua is speaking Greek with the pair) when disgusted angels intervene:

> "Let them enjoy themselves; if you have any bad feeling between you, forgive each other." Then they goaded the pair, and they said to Optatus, "Get your people in line, because they meet with you as if they were fans coming back from the chariot races and brawling over the different teams." And so it seemed to us as if they wanted to close the gates.[21]

Saturus is showing delicately that the angels shut out these irritations. Before awakening with joy, he sees familiar "brothers" and even martyrs known to him. He and his friend are in company who understand how they feel and what they have been through.

Neither Perpetua nor Saturus has any taste for the relatively abstract and sublimated heaven of the New Testament, the apostolic fathers, or the church fathers. Their heaven is a return to the best parts of childhood, which have few literary resonances before the *Suffering*. This would be a childhood more like Perpetua's, and less like that of the two slaves or any freedmen in the group: being indulged, getting the better of challenges without having to worry about them, taking in the beauty of nature, playing without pressure, enjoying friendship unimpeded.

My forays into modern studies of dreaming did little to further my understanding of Perpetua's dreams. I ended up relying on some of the most general findings, which hardly needed research: dreams have strange and seemingly inconsequential elements, but they do reflect experience, and thus they characterize individual dreamers; sometimes they are revelatory. Perpetua's visions are an unusually convincing and moving combination. There is the ordinary, quirky, opaque kind of dreaming, recollections from which are notoriously

I Knew I Spoke with the Master

boring and irritating to listen to; there is content such as people usually shrink from sharing, because it is too revealing about themselves; and there are glorious or shattering visions tantamount to those reported in sacred literature for the purpose of addressing great problems of existence.

What, then, do Perpetua's dreams show about her? First of all, they are honest; it is hard to imagine her making them up. Even the most expansive visions of previous Christian literature show tight thematic control; they may have a basis in reality, but they do not seem like what somebody actually dreamed, whereas Perpetua's dreams do. She stares at weapons and torture instruments, anguishes over a beloved, unbaptized dead brother stranded outside the heaven she seeks, struggles to reach the place of testing, and arrives out of breath. Her real concerns and limitations pass into her revelations as if through an underground stream.

In addition, the dreams are grounded in the human world. In none of her four dreams does heavenly power reach down when Perpetua is frightened or anguished. Her cause would be lost without the help of friendly mentors or (in the case of her dead brother's plight) her own characteristically brash initiative. Presiding and welcoming figures that do represent divinity (the shepherd, the referee in the arena, the throned Christ) are firmly embodied. Human or humanlike beings, not a disembodied divinity or his immortal servants in uncanny (if any) forms, move the heroine forward and provide her with a resting place.

The dreams also, of course, show Perpetua's egotism. The mainstream literature of martyrdom loves gestures of self-erasure. With vehemence, a martyr threatened with praise will give all the credit to Christ, and self-protective modesty seems normal in this fraught realm. If I dreamed of being the star among some chosen few religious champions, and the darling of heaven, I would keep the dream to myself. The story of Joseph and his brothers gives no negligible warning: he dreams they bow down to him, he tells them about the dream, and he barely survives to regret his choice. But Perpetua's premise at the start for purposeful dreaming, that the other favors from God that she has enjoyed assure her of prophetic power, apparently buoys her in accepting what she sees in sleep or a semi-conscious state as true and holy, no matter how flattering it is to her, and to be shared without embarrassment. Again, this is only as far as the extant text goes. It would be impossible to guess what self-censorship or editorial selection changed the original text; none of the dreams looks incomplete, but some real but uninspired ones may be missing from her account.

As to the rarest qualities of her dreams, their dynamism and dramatic rounding that give the feel of life-altering or purpose-confirming revelation, I need to beg readers' indulgence and contrast a routine nightmare of my own with one that took an extraordinary turn. Last week I dreamed I could not find the room for an exam I needed to pass to graduate from college, then I could not find the questions within the ten-page handout, then I could not read the questions in their Gothic font, and then when I deciphered them I realized that they were not for the course I had taken, but I still had to pass this exam. The proctor treated me as a nuisance; I was trying to plan what to do with my failed life, but my mind wouldn't work.

I think this is typical of ordinary dreams; they are supposed to have magical qualities because their formation is mysterious, but in reality most are quite flat. We feel more or less the same way throughout them, fearful or confused or ashamed or at best reassured or hopeful in some qualified way. If it is true that dreams are a means of psychic resolution, I call them a pageantry of failure, like Edwardian flying machines crumbling over cliffs and docks in

I Knew I Spoke with the Master

black-and-white montage footage. I have often watched my dog dreaming, and he never catches up with the rabbit or squirrel or sheep or whatever it is he is running after and snapping at in his head; he never wakes up content with not being allowed to hunt or herd. Dreams almost never shape up.

But I experienced one great exception during a time of enormous stress. In the dream, I was looking for the exam registration venue in a very unfriendly molded concrete building, and no one would listen to my plea for directions. At last, when I saw by a clock that I was forty minutes late already, I sat down on a cold white step and sobbed. Then there was someone sitting by my side, a young man I didn't dare look in the face, who told me not to be concerned, he would tell me what I needed to know, and he began to speak. I am not sure that, even in sleep, I took in any of his words; my overwhelming memory is that he cared for me, for my mind and my future. I identified him with Jesus and told Christian friends about the dream, which excited them. Later I included this dream in a poem, which was published to a good response. The dream was an important part of my life and became a small part of collective memory because it had narrative direction, a point, and a use.

All of Perpetua's reported dreaming is like this, dramatic and shapely. She was — astonishingly for someone who counts, by our reckoning, as inexperienced and narrow, even shallow — able to work her way through the problems of terror, grief, and her own death and come up with satisfactory psychic solutions, adjusting alien and awkward elements to suit herself. Saturus's reported dream (to which I do suspect she contributed) is comparatively shapeless. It is entirely about joyous deliverance and welcome, glory, reunion, and pleasure; it has no suspense. The most believable thing about it is the intrusion in heaven of the still-living quarrelsome church officials, whom the angels scold, urging one of them to repress the rowdy behavior that plainly still worries Saturus as he takes his leave of earthly responsibilities. But the dream does not process much; it is a happy one from beginning to end, and momentary problems fall into the care of the heavenly authorities. In Perpetua's dreams the resolutions come too quickly and easily, but there *are* plots, with huge tensions to be dealt with. On the evidence of later works they inspired, these stories entered more fully into collective memory, culture, and religion than most other parts of the *Suffering* did. Yet to all appearances, she did not contrive or invent them but produced the whole sequence in her unconscious or partly conscious mind through the promptings of her immediate circle, her trying circumstances, religious traditions that were new to her, and her own formidable will. She takes things that are in some cases literally earthy, like the ground the snake is lying on, the dirt on her little brother's clothes, and the sand rubbed on a wrestler's body, and *connects* them to the heights of heaven through her own congenial logic. She was an artist of spirituality, confident enough to let us see her faults, hearty enough to conceive and articulate a lasting world.

I cannot resist a sort of footnote here. Whereas the prison narrative links the *Suffering* across the centuries to modern women's writing, Perpetua's and Saturus's dreams may more properly be categorized as the first young people's literature. Unlike women's writing, this literature does not probe the meaning of limitations; it vaults over them with the imagination because limitations are intolerable. Scholars usually locate the "invention" of childhood, adolescence, and post-adolescence, and their literature, in the early-modern period, when prolonged education and delayed marriage allowed young people to linger over their own existential questions. But Romans with secure means had long been educating sons with great elaboration and putting their marriages off far into adulthood; nearly all girls were married before their early twenties, but Perpetua provides just one example of a female whose education went well beyond the skills and knowledge suited to an obscure domestic role.

Furthermore, when Christianity was threatening to break up the heavy structure of Roman social and intellectual authority, young people found important chances at self-expression. The questions raised sidelong in the *Suffering* are not alien to what certain institutions and media were asking a great deal later. If the fate of the young is not at the center of the moral universe, then why not? If those who are coming of age or a little older take on an outsize proportion of a society's sufferings and sacrifices, why aren't they admitted to a discussion of what this means? And what is wrong with aspiring to a world that is more like a happy child's, more trusting, more loving, and more carefree?

The Roman Empire's coming throes, and the steady authoritarian tendency of Christianity before the modern era, prevented these concerns from blossoming. But that one young woman and her male friend managed to get them across in the approach to martyrdom — whose tropes are among the most rigid and artificial in religious literature — and to do it with enough verve that their impressions survived the coming long theocratic crackdown, is an achievement of rare interest.

CHAPTER FIVE

Fattened for a Sacrifice to Caesar

Perpetua was, in many ways, a living message. The early parts of her narrative and her dreams weigh toward soulful brashness and urge the conclusion that the narrator is a real person in a real if ecstatic plight. But that does not do away with the sense that this real person edited herself and was edited by other people. Her words and behavior were shaped in an attempt to keep her story within the bounds of martyrdom as a literary genre and an established ritual. I have already pointed out, for example, how the textual Perpetua returns to meek, pious, and communal language after flights of self-assertive inspiration.

Adding to such layers, which make it hard enough to learn anything solid about her, she performs and is directed as a performer in a forum very hostile to Christians: the Roman arena games. The common mistake in her own time and long afterward was to see her as a pure victim. And in our day, it is apparently tempting to concoct a Hollywood version of martyrdom with her as a star, a tale of heroic innocence versus decadent cruelty, the power of the spirit versus material power. But that formula — I choose the word advisedly because it is used for fiction with a single controlling idea—does not leave sufficient room for what contemporary Christians actually did and said, and especially not for how at times they turned the games into their own popular communication medium.

Exponents of early Christianity are fond of saying that the movement was "radical," but they do not go into the full implications of how radical movements work (despite a great deal of evidence in the modern world), let alone how Christians coped at the time. These early adherents frankly called some of their tactics warfare, and the hard facts show that they enthusiastically engaged in asymmetrical information warfare as well as the literal violence of the arena. This in itself makes for an awkward interpretive challenge, but in addition, Roman officials and organizers of the games (not identical groups) had their own complex and only partly revealed interests, which might put them on the Christians' side and pit them against one another at certain junctures.

Since Christians' deaths were both crimes committed and punishments meted out by the justice system, and since the victims stressed the idea of themselves as living and dying testimony ("martyr" comes from the Greek word for a witness in court), I cannot see a better way forward than to try to work things out logically, as in a courtroom, based on what the parties do and say and what they do not—in this case, mostly not. Scenes of Perpetua's own and her friends' deaths in the arena, and of the lead-up to the spectacle, abound with blanks and conundrums. To speculate about exactly what did happen, let alone why, is to sway at the edge of a biographical cliff. In my biography of Vergil, I felt I could speculate about certain turns of events (always identifying the speculation as such) because the evidence of his writings and of his social and historical context is massive, though personal information about him is skimpy.

But for Perpetua, most of what we have is truth claims that do not fit together. They demand extra-careful consideration.

So I am going to avoid any attempt at a large synthesis. After a brief historical summary, I will highlight parts of the *Suffering* narrative that most strikingly fail to match up with what we "know" about other games and other arena martyrdoms, and the parts that are least consistent with each other or internally.

Spectators of arena games were more select than the crowds at the other mass-audience sport, chariot racing. The latter offered a great deal more space for seating because of the very long track, and men and women of all classes were allowed to sit together, whereas for blood sports (and dramas) the seating was reserved and segregated. Chariot racing was a more ordinary sport, like footraces or modern baseball, whereas the amphitheater games were an occasion on which civil society dealt out violence under fixed auspices. Both were public entertainments (in effect, bribes for votes and other political support, and a distraction for bored and restless urbanites), requiring moneyed sponsorship either public or private and introduced by parades and other ceremonies. By its nature, chariot racing did not lend itself to new, spectacular effects and explosively competitive spending; and mayhem, while it might happen, was not an essential part of the program.

The games were the country of brutal artifice, where virtually anything could happen if there was the will to make it happen — fantasy battles and even sea battles, or the emperor himself killing a rhino. The games laid down the rule of the exceptional: the audience felt entitled to see one gladiator emerge from prolonged and ingenious slaughter without a fatal or disabling wound. This was an apt scene to which Christians, who believed that they alone could conquer death through faith, could bring their transformative ambition, following up for the first time their private meetings with a public enactment of who they were.

It is plain why the games in turn wanted Christians. Roman games had three standard parts: the wild beast hunt in the morning, the execution of condemned prisoners around midday, and the gladiator contests in the afternoon. The need for spectacle inflation plagued the organizers throughout the early Christian era. All kinds of exotic animals were pitted against each other or killed by hunters, sometimes with new techniques or apparatus. Wild beasts might kill the condemned as well (who might be immobilized on special platforms or scaffolding or in nets), and fiendish devices like metal roasting chairs might torment them, elaborating the relatively neglected and scorned midday show, which intersected with the time for lunch and the customary nap. Gladiators, with their traditional equipment (heavy and light armor and weapons in various national or pseudo-national styles) and maneuvers (exhausting a massive, metal-laden combatant by skipping ahead of him under the hot sun was a ready defense, as in the amphitheater scene in the film *The Life of Brian*), labored under demands for improved skills and thrills within a regulation framework. Gladiator games apparently started as funeral entertainment, and war captives sometimes reenacted their army's defeat, but later investment in regular, blockbuster professional shows set much higher standards. The novelist Petronius lampoons a freedman connoisseur of games, keen for first-class slaughter and scornful of fighters worse than "people thrown to the animals."[1] Naturally, elements of the more prestigious and suspenseful gladiator fights as well as of the exotic beast hunts might leech into the executions: a condemned prisoner might, for instance, be provided with some kind of inferior weapon with which to delay death, and his chances of a reprieve — such as a brave but losing gladiator might hope for — might be raised above zero.

Fattened for a Sacrifice to Caesar

The resources needed to keep up with splashy innovations demanded by the public were, obviously, limited. Wild animal numbers fell short; the Roman games are the main reason that lions, elephants, and other iconic species became rare or nonexistent in North Africa and the Near East, as opposed to places bounty hunters could not reach; and it was difficult and expensive to find, catch, transport, keep alive, and train wild animals even when they were plentiful. The novelist Apuleius depicts a rich man's extensive bear collection, into which he has sunk a large part of his fortune, dying of disease before he can feature it in his important production.[2] Incidental details about games suggest the use of animals that did not readily attack humans, either because these were not the right species — few actually exist — or because specimens that might have been aggressive were terrified, weak, or sick: the bear that is supposed to attack Saturus in the *Suffering* will not come out of its cage.[3] The ferocious "cow" sicced against Perpetua and Felicitas in section 20 sounds like a comical expedient. Ascription of anything to the devil in martyr literature should be a red flag: the narrator does not want to go into the genuine dynamics of events and falls back on good-and-evil duality; here, the devil is said to have supplied the cow. Even substituting "the organizers" for the devil would not make sense of the choice (which the narrator admits is unusual) of a female animal to attack females. This is probably not Bossy the sweet Guernsey milker; there are (or were) hulking indigenous North African bovines that were not to be toyed with, whether male or female. But I strongly suspect that the procurers of animals simply could not come up with the expected bull; the normal number of mature bulls in a herd was one, and deprived of its bull, a herd could not reproduce; bulls are also much harder to catch and handle. This cow was likely among the beasts that handlers had to goad, whip, or singe in arenas to move them toward their targets; however motivated, she does not get the job done: she fails to knock the women down so hard that they cannot stand up together. Once they do, the cow, if still on the loose, drops out of notice. Maybe some stage manager chased her with a rope or something, but as with the other animals when not in action, what happens to the cow is not supposed to matter in the story presented.

But the *audience* finds the *pair of women* riveting; this is apparently the moment when popular sensation turns from hostility to mercy: the women are dramatically reprieved. In reading of turns in the action like this, you can almost feel the tastes of spectators and the calculations of showmen ticking over. Multiplying and elaborating the deaths of common criminals as the main attraction might seem a cheap and easy alternative to acquiring skilled gladiators and rare beasts, but common criminals were not always on hand. Slaves had practically no legal rights and could be tortured and killed whether they had done anything wrong or not, but slaves were vital commodities, not to be thrown away extravagantly. Attractive, appealing slaves, whose fate an audience cared more about, were naturally more valuable, and they carried their former masters' reputation with them to their deaths. (Echion, the games critic in the *Satyricon*, is disgusted with the *owner* of an adulterous slave who sent him to the arena.)[4] Gladiators, with their prolonged training, were among the more expensive slaves, and winners were entitled to prize money, and retirement if they had a run of wins.

Christians, in contrast, were not hard to find, and they cost nothing; some even turned themselves in. A short hearing with a yes-or-no question about affiliation sufficed for their condemnation, after which the only expense and trouble were their maintenance in jail until the big event. And they provided superb dramatic displays. They came from all walks of life but the loftiest; they might be respectable and law-abiding except for their disreputable

Fattened for a Sacrifice to Caesar

"superstition," which they considered more important than their lives, so spectators could thrill to the challenge of breaking down their self-assurance and shudder at the peril of their ways. The guard who taunts Felicitas during her labor relishes the thought of her tortured and dying because he judges her reckless in her refusal to perform a pagan sacrifice, and arrogant in her scorn of the wild animals. In another key scene, the producers of the games, assuming that the audience wants to see the two women sexually degraded, cause them to be led out, naked and restrained in nets, as victims for the wild cow — then, after the attack, comes the heady, admiring reprieve.[5] Christians were good material.

Christians cooperated by becoming good material. Our popular influences would have us picture the Roman state ferreting out Christians aggressively and making examples of them just because they were a counterculture, but Pliny's correspondence with the emperor Trajan testifies to a policy of fairness and restraint; the paucity of extant pagan discussions of Christianity during these early centuries shows how little interest elite Romans had in the sect per se. Christianity was illegal for what the Roman regime tended to articulate as law-and-order reasons, and Christians would have found it fairly easy to lie low. Sacrifices for the emperor's welfare, which Christians rejected as idolatrous, were intended to enact civic loyalty and conformity; hence the demand at a hearing for a sacrifice as proof that the accused was not Christian — but this was only when an accusation came to a head; there was no prior, intrusive regulation of religion.

Romans tended to suspect large private gatherings of having seditious purposes, and Christians had no temples, and as yet no churches, for their worship; they crowded into the home of the most well-to-do and influential Christian in the district, exciting neighbors' suspicions. Accordingly, rumors puffed up Christian language — the "love feast" of "brothers and sisters," the ritual "eating of flesh and drinking of blood" — into evidence of mass depravity that threatened the whole polity. But for a long period Roman officials appear to have rarely treated accused Christians according to these terms. Instead, their actions were in line with Pliny's findings (or the results of their own investigations): there was nothing to support the scandal-mongering. Trajan, in accord with his deputy Pliny, ruled against actively hunting Christians down, accepting anonymous denunciations, or punishing anyone who recanted. Christian accounts themselves, especially those with a version of transcripts, confirm this restraint down the generations: officials did not *want* to issue condemnations; they urged the easy ritual off-ramp on the accused and were angry when they would not take it. The magistrate who condemns Perpetua and her friends is, like her father, exasperated enough with Christian stubbornness that he resorts to violence.[6]

But the use of Christians in public entertainments points to a big exception, a whole public realm where another attitude prevailed. The text of the *Suffering* suggests that organizers of the games made special arrangements for presenting the Perpetuan martyrs, and perhaps even worked with them and their supporters to craft a performance that would have the most stirring effect. (Of course, Christians and the Roman establishment had very different messages to deliver through the performance, but this consideration would not have prevented either side from striving, in coordinated competition, to deliver its own message through the single event.) This dynamic may eventually have come full circle and influenced the justice (or injustice) system itself, which would help explain the harsher and more sweeping persecutions reported over time, culminating in the emperor Diocletian's purges in the early fourth century. As hunting more ingeniously and farther afield would have produced more animals for the arena, more ruthless legal measures would have produced more Christians for it.

It is at any rate evident that Christian bodies were there when the Roman hierarchy needed them. This was so for the first mass persecution in the year 64, in which Nero scapegoated Christians for the Great Fire of Rome and deployed them as human torches at a nighttime festival in public places. He could have readily sourced his Christians (real or merely accused) from the same local gossip and feud machines that made them (like other vulnerable people) easy to lay hands on.

From the Christian side, martyrdom had obvious practical benefits. Christians might cherish their community and believe fervently in their special calling and destiny, but frustration with their obscurity was likely to mount. The Second Coming had not happened, many generations after it was prophesied. Converts did come, but they did not belong to the upper crust. Christianity was making history only by the persecutions that registered through public events. Hence when a martyr was merely put to the sword (for example, Cyprian, a bishop of Carthage, was beheaded in 258), the event was apparently treated at the time and certainly rendered in the literature of martyrdom as conspicuous and momentous, following the important models of idealistic Roman suicides like those of Lucretia and Cato the Younger. When Tertullian declared that the blood of martyrs was the seed of the church, he was admitting that the church (in the Bible an "assembly" of believers, the Greek word pointing to a *public* assembly) was embryonic, and demanding that it grow to prominence even at the cost of lives.[7] Other early Christian authors, such as Minucius Felix, agreed on the glory—and the necessity—of the martyrdom spectacle. If this principle does not make sense out of the whole *Suffering* text — and it certainly does not — it does give a premise for questions that are more than merely bland or pious.

These questions are as basic as geography. Were Perpetua and her friends residents of Thuburbo Minus, as several versions of the story claim? If not, where does the claim come from? A standard proviso for reading ancient texts is that "the more difficult reading is the stronger one"; as Agatha Christie's Hercule Poirot would insist, an incongruous clue should be taken seriously, not jammed in to "fit" with other facts that may themselves have been falsified in order to support each other. The redactor of the Latin *Suffering* wants us to picture a prominent Carthaginian lady, but her father does not behave, and is not treated, as if he commands anything, not even the means to get his daughter under control, and he is beaten in public by the province's ruler, an indignity from which a Roman citizen should have been exempt. Obscure and petty Thuburban origins would also help explain why his daughter is subjected to a cruel and degrading execution. Moreover, the only previous report of a Christian prosecution in North Africa is in the *town* of Scillium. Were the members of Perpetua's group victims and performers of convenience, all sourced from middling to lower classes in a backwater? If so, their celebrity far outclassed their origins; the whole group was, among other honors, eventually memorialized by a basilica at Carthage. Did this will to enlarge infect everyone's behavior, as well as the written record, from the start? Were pagan showmen as well as Christian believers in on the enlargement, doing their part to turn a cheap, ad hoc show into an unforgettable drama?

If a sentence of the *Suffering*'s text is correct, Perpetua died not in the amphitheater outside Carthage (one of the biggest in the Roman Empire) but in an amphitheater attached to a military base, to which the prisoners were moved before the games.[8] Military camps could have their own amphitheaters; they had many of the amenities of cities. But the building in the *Suffering* is large enough for the crowd to demand that the prisoners be brought into the center for a better view of their deaths.[9] If the location is the regional military headquarters for the Third Legion, that would be several days' journey inland from Carthage. (Inland tribes threatened the wealthy, Romanized African coastal regions; Roman armies were regularly stationed for frontier defense) Would the interim provincial governor, Hilarianus, who presides over the games, celebrate the imperial prince's birthday there, and not in the provincial capital? Most of the details in the text in fact point to Carthage, but then why does Perpetua say they were transferred to the camp for its own games — an emphatic statement, its Latin literally referencing both the "base's prison" and the "base's games"? Are the games, as well as the doomed performers in them, shown elsewhere in the text to be more important than they were?

To explore this possibility, let me look at some major discrepancies one by one from the start of the *Suffering* narrative. Whereas the redactor, at the beginning of the story in section 2, frankly states that the five Christians he names were "arrested" or caught, he leaves out all the specific circumstances and turns instantly to Perpetua's respectability and her own authorship of the writing that follows. Perpetua, or the Perpetua of the text, cooperates thoroughly in denying the martyrdom a backstory and certifying that she is a conventionally admirable person, a conscientious mother (to the extent she can manage), and tender-hearted and family-minded — so much so that she takes her influence with God to heroic lengths to obtain baptism for her dead brother. But in the reality behind this edifying content, there are only three possibilities for how the group came into the authorities' hands: a civilian or civilians turned them in, they turned themselves in, or Roman officials took the initiative in hunting them down.

To admit that someone who knew them turned them in would clash with the church's insistence on martyrs' blessedness and holiness; they were not ordinary human beings, subject to ordinary resentments, machinations, feuds, or their own indiscreet behavior. Their enemy was the devil, but he cannot feature in such a realistic story as Perpetua's. The second path toward martyrdom, turning oneself in, would be an even trickier one to handle narratively. The act verges on suicide, an ethical matter on which Christians diverged decisively from pagans; choices that resembled suicide could bring martyrdom into question even among Christians. And for their part, pagans were inclined to treat Christians' volunteering to die as ridiculous, not noble, because the cause was not country or honor or escape from a less dignified death: the cause was invisible, so the volunteers must be insane. The third possibility, which would entail organized, policy-driven religious policing on the part of the state, is the least likely: there is little or no evidence that such policing occurred at this stage of history. But granted that it did occur, Christian authors would have by no means been apt to depict Roman authorities acting in this cruel and intrusive way. Christianity's political defense of itself was the opposite: the sect was thoroughly law-abiding and loyal to Roman imperial power, under which God's providence had placed it; it was the devil's machinations and not any wrongdoing of Roman officials – who were just doing their God-given jobs – that caused the torment and death of Christians. In sum, then, the *Suffering* was not permitted to include any causal rationale that may have been available for the main events it narrates; hence the starkly minimalist narrative.

The guards of those under Roman house arrest were regularly called "attendants" as if they were a protective escort; there is nothing unusual about Perpetua calling them that where her house arrest is concerned. But the ordinary Latin word for "guards" never comes up later in the story, where it would belong, and no wonder: guards are for wrongdoers and the weak and unreliable. Juvenal's famous question, "Who's going to guard those guards of yours?" is about corruptible slaves set to watch over women prone to adultery.[10] Most personnel in the prison and at the games in the *Suffering* are singled out as members of the military: adjutant, tribune, soldier. Especially insofar as they are converts or potential converts, this falls in with the imagery of the martyr as a brave and dutiful soldier and a champion in the battle with the devil. The exception can be found among Perpetua's shocked and distressed words about the experience of landing in jail: soldiers are shaking the group down.[11] This is a sentence to bear in mind, coming as it does after her tough-minded first face-off with her father. She does not simply get and stay brave after her conversion. Acting out and relating irreconcilable versions of her story creates evident strain, which will evidently catch up with her.

The term for the group's transfer to the jail is *recipimur* (literally, "we are received"): when used of taking a person into a place, it usually connotes refuge, hospitality, or recognition of status. My attempt at a catch-all in the translation is "taken in [at]." Perpetua virtually casts herself as a well-treated diplomatic hostage in wartime, who would be guest in an elite home. But the alarmed recounting of jail conditions interrupts.

As transactors for the better conditions and the temporary release, the government side is not named; the Christian ministers seemingly deal with no one.[12] Later, no individuals perform the function of taking the prisoners roughly and hurriedly to the forum for their decisive hearing: they are "seized" (a passive verb) there from their lunch.[13] Perpetua never uses verbs of forceful confinement, even when she and the others are locked in the stocks: they literally "stay" or "remain" there, a word that could be used for sojourning as a guest.

Specific interactions with jail personnel exclude almost everything but respect for the Christians or fear of them. The head of the jail, the adjutant Pudens (Modest) comes into the narrative only after Perpetua's third dream, and only to "make much of" the Christians. Understanding their "great power" he lets in many people, but the verb is *admitto,* the same one that could be used for a majordomo letting in select visitors to some important person.[14] An unnamed military tribune restricts the group in dread of their rumored magic powers but then shudders and turns red at Perpetua's fearless, witty upbraiding; the result is better treatment and comforting visitors, Christians and (curiously) others; the adjutant is now a convert and does not stand in the way.[15]

Accordioned together like this, the narrative makes little sense. Prisoners in a Roman jail could hardly subsist without an ongoing quid pro quo to allow the delivery of necessities (there was, needless to say, no cafeteria, no infirmary, no laundry), but after the bribe for better quarters recorded in section 3, no quid is ever mentioned; instead, the impression is that the group is allowed any number of visitors just by being holy and standing on their dignity. Historically, soldiers seem to have been apt converts to Christianity, but this cannot be the whole story.

The most sweeping apparent rewriting in the *Suffering,* however, is the upgrade from an execution of prisoners to a gladiatorial contest. I have shown how Perpetua's fourth vision takes her two giant steps up the ladder of respect, showing her not as a gladiator but as a competitor in the sport of wrestling, for many centuries the basis of the elite Greek training of male youth. She triumphs yet avoids the brutality of the pankration bout by rising in the air and kicking.

Fattened for a Sacrifice to Caesar

She also is shown getting away, and more than getting away, with presenting herself as a gladiator with a gladiator's prerogatives: in rhetorically brilliant but hugely overstated sallies, she lays claim to the food that will allow her to perform at her best in honor of Caesar, and to the "contract" the group has made in order to appear.[16]

But actual events may have assisted both her and her literary presenters to create confusion about her role and her experience. Did this group of the condemned get special treatment and choice billing because there were two young women in it, one of them from a respectable family? Or was an execution extravaganza routinely replacing beast hunts and gladiator combats? What role did the unpopularity or notoriety or impressiveness, the stoicism or enthusiasm of Christians play?

Be all of that as it may, one thing in the *Suffering* that is striking — but should not be surprising — is the adoption and large-scale validation of the culture of the games by Christians. In this narrative the games culture all but drowns out any distinctly Christian biblical or moral or theological elements. This is not because Perpetua and other contributors to the *Suffering* were not single-mindedly committed to their religion; the facts speak for themselves on that score. Rather, the religion was not fully formed. It did not yet have its own established, authoritative culture — nothing to compare with what the Roman Empire delivered routinely and prestigiously. Therefore, Christians used elements of pagan culture for their own purposes. For example, two hundred years after the events of the *Suffering*, Augustine found himself combating the continuation of pagan rites with Christian labels slapped on them, such as food and drink offerings to the dead that allowed for cemetery picnics; he had an uphill battle, because the church provided no festivities that could compete in meaningfulness and congeniality for ordinary Christians.

Perpetua

It is not remarkable that Perpetua and her companions and supporters in martyrdom used the cultural resources they had available to express themselves. It *is* remarkable that Perpetua manages to glory in these resources and blend them exuberantly, along with her new faith, into her own vivid personality. But as the narrative draws toward a close, the strain shows more and more. The games are not just a means of presenting herself and what she believes in; they are also the instrument of her death. But she is constrained to deny this: the Christian teaching she has embraced insists that they are the gateway to eternal life. The degree of denial required would have been beyond the power of any fundamentally frank and sensitive person, and it is shown eventually taking its toll.

She and her friends partake of the banquet given to gladiators on the night before the games. I would lean toward this as a historical reality, because it happened in public, with spectators who would remember it; and pagan handlers of the Christians, for their part, could make the usual use of it as an extension of the games. That the pagans simply acceded to their admiration of the Christians and changed arrangements that had suited them before (as claimed in sections 9 and 16 of the *Suffering*) looks like a stretch. But the reality of condemned Christians feasting the way gladiators did would have intriguing implications. If professional gladiators were to fight in these games, they could not have appreciated religious criminals and arena amateurs basking in the publicity and enjoying the luxuries of what was their own potential last meal, a traditional prerogative; even if the gladiators got a duplicate last meal elsewhere, the Christians cut into their attention. Does it follow that there were no gladiators slated for these games, and that the Christians began their ordeals as soon as they arrived in the morning, instead of waiting for the midday execution show? That is what the text seems to show, but the Christian version would understandably resist giving them rivals for the popular gaze; and is it believable that Carthage celebrated the birthday of the emperor's son with executions alone? In any event, a showy dinner party could not have been the optimal preparation for a sheltered, already overconfident young woman who was to face a bloody ordeal.

The usual spectators arrive at the dining facility, but Saturus tells them off, mocking them in their contrasting roles as fascinated gawkers and lethal enemies, and warning them to "take a good look and remember our faces": Judgment Day is coming for them, and Saturus anticipates that he and his friends will be judges. That the gawkers went away stunned is plausible; that many converted on the basis of this one encounter is not. The passage does, however, credibly convey the psychology of a radical movement: everything is obliged to work in its favor toward the inevitable end of combined power and righteousness. But Perpetua is left uncharacteristically silent—either because male voices are taking over in the text (her writing ends six sections before this) or were taking over in reality, or because the real Perpetua had become less communicative.

In the text the group of martyrs dominates the spectacles on the day of the games. No one else appears in the parade—no other acts, no dignitaries, no one but the joyous comrades. The male martyrs seem to act as a sort of entourage, walking before the two women, the star being of course Perpetua, "the lawful wife of Christ, ... the pampered darling of God," whom everyone stares at, but who stares back so that all avert their eyes.[17]

Once she is before the crowd, she is depicted for the first time as a sexual creature. She is someone to stare at and provoke to stare back, and to picture in erotic relationships with the divinities for whom she is about to die. The playful or ironic vocabulary from this Christian source is disturbing, and may even hint at Christians' cooperation with pagan showmen in offering her for titillation. The insensitivity may subsist only in these words written and circulated after the fact, but the words contrast with her own clear testimony as to how she saw herself, as a Christian rewarded for the ultimate sacrifice by the privilege of spending eternity as a sexless, cherished daughter and a joyful child. She is in fact correct about her religion, and the male Christian sentiment that puts her on display as the imagined snuggle bunny of heavenly powers outrages the basic theology that those transformed by the Spirit leave behind the conflicts and burdens of the flesh, especially sexuality. If Perpetua was feeling such outrage toward the spectators who ogled her, no wonder she gave them a strong, intimidating stare.

Felicitas in her turn is endowed with a baroque sexist metaphor: her martyrdom sees her going blissfully "from blood to blood, from the midwife to the gladiator who fights with a net, about to wash after birth with a second baptism."[18] But she clearly does not want womanhood, childbirth, or motherhood to be interwoven and identified with herself as she faces death; while still pregnant, she prayed to be past these things, and she went cheerfully through physical torments so that her prayer could be granted.

Perpetua does speak up, and does sound like herself, as she resists the demand that the prisoners put on the costumes of pagan priests and devotees. She borrows for herself and her companions all the dignity of a citizen with uncompromised liberty and all the prerogatives of a gladiator.[19]

I chortle grimly at a P. C. Vey cartoon with a thought balloon above flailing human limbs and two predators intently at work: "I thought being eaten by wolves would be different." For someone like Perpetua especially, no preparation for deadly violence can really suffice. In the text, the artifices of celebrity and the illusions they give of protection begin to come apart soon after the games open. Entering the arena, she is singing a hymn, lost in her own world: her song is about stamping on the Egyptian's head. But Revocatus, Saturninus, and Saturus—the increasingly outspoken males—threaten the audience; when they pass by Hilarianus's seat and make menacing gestures at him, the crowd has had enough. The punishment demanded is for the prisoners to run the gauntlet down the ranks of whip-wielding animal handlers. A defiant response is recorded: the group is jubilant at sharing one of Christ's tribulations. But I can imagine that Perpetua was shaken. Had anyone whipped her in her life?[20]

Then, in section 19, the scene shifts to the adolescent posturing of the men, who have earlier discussed which wild animals they wanted to encounter, Saturninus figuring that his heavenly reward would be more glorious if he encounters them all, Saturus wishing to die from one bite of the leopard because he hates bears. Their wishes begin to play out.

Yet in section 20, Perpetua, along with Felicitas, is sinking into helplessness, possibly with some accompaniments of farce. She has spurned the pagan costumes and gotten away with it, but now nothing prevents the stripping of both women; wrapped only in a net, they are presented to the "monstrously fierce" . . . cow. Their "stripping" is conveyed by a term that can apply to warriors: *despoliatae*. The martial image would convey armor taken off them after their deaths on the battlefield. This seems almost mocking to me, as the more acute humiliation of female nakedness is visited on the pair, and they are still alive to feel it. Even more troubling, "stripping" (or "plundering") can be an erotic metaphor in pagan literature: the lover's finery is removed, and some may be kept as a souvenir. The crowd's protests, not Perpetua's this time, restore their dignity. As I argued above, the cow is probably a cheap, tormented substitute for a bull. The women, unlike the men, give no sign of being in a sporting mood.

Perpetua

Section 20 conveys that the moment Perpetua is knocked down and wounded brings a plunge into horror that her conscious mind cannot sustain. The details in this description carry great importance.

> Perpetua was tossed first, and landed on her backside. Then when she sat up, she pulled her tunic, which had been torn down the side, back over her to cover her thigh, more conscious of modesty than pain. Next she asked for a clip and pinned up her disordered hair: it was not seemly for a female martyr to have disheveled hair while she was suffering, in case she seemed to be mourning when she was actually in her glory. Then she got up and, when she saw that Felicitas had been slammed down, she went over to her, took her by the hand, and helped her to her feet. Then the two stood side by side. But the hardheartedness of the crowd was overcome, and the two were called back to the Gate of Life. There Perpetua was taken over by a certain candidate for baptism named Rusticus, who was attached to her. She was roused from a sort of sleep (she was so deep in the spirit and in a trance) and began to look around her, and to the surprise of everyone, said, "When do we get brought out to that cow sort of thing?" And when she was told that this had already happened, she wouldn't believe it until she recognized on her body and clothes certain marks from the tossing. After that, her brother and the above-mentioned candidate for baptism were summoned, and she addressed them, saying, "Stand fast in your faith, and love one another, all of you, and do not let our sufferings set a trap for you."[21]

The narrator cannot, of course, know what she is feeling and puts the most sanctimonious glosses on her actions. Modesty — or rather shame — would be a natural response of such a person to a leg exposed to a crowd of gawking strangers, but Perpetua has been hurt,

Fattened for a Sacrifice to Caesar

as will quickly become clear: the cow has left marks on her. Her first impulse should be to look or clutch at whatever part of her body took the impact. But it will also soon become clear that she cannot feel the damage. She is in shock or is dissociating, or both.

Such a state would be consistent with her pausing to fix her hair as well as cover her thigh with her torn skirt while her companion lies on the ground, having been struck too hard to get up on her own. Incidentally, it seems bizarre that anyone near her would have a hair clip on hand, or would go and fetch one. And from where? Did not Carthage share the regulation that women must be seated high up on the stands? But maybe Perpetua retrieves her own hair clip, which has fallen off. The Latin verb used here, *requiro,* can means a physical action, "try to find": the image would be of her groping around in the sand for her lost accessary – not unthinkable at this very disorienting point in her ordeal, but unlikely as what the Christian author wanted to convey.

Any attention she would have paid to her hair at this point looks like an attempt to retreat to a lost sense of superiority and control. Hairstyles were an important display of a Roman matron's status, and an art to which they submitted at considerable cost of time and thought. In her home, Perpetua would have routinely chosen a hairstyle and kept an eye on the skilled slave woman crafting it, and when she entertained or went out, her coiffure would signal that she was worth the trouble. Christians for their part condemned hairstyles, even braiding, but women's hair *was* supposed to be confined or veiled, out of the way and not trailing, which had erotic implications. Whichever standards were uppermost in Perpetua's consciousness, to have her hair hanging down in odd strands in public may have been a more nightmarish sensation, more an attack on her sense of self, than to be knocked to the ground and hurt by an animal, because she had never devoted any care to avoiding that.

Perpetua

Perpetua manages to stand, and helps Felicitas up. The crowd relents, and the two women are called to the Gate of Life; they seem to have a reprieve. Perpetua is caught up by Rusticus, a candidate for baptism who "was attached to her" (or "was clinging to her" or "was a loyal supporter of hers"), and she awakens "from a sort of sleep" to ask in dismissive terms about the pending attack ("When do we get brought out to that cow sort of thing?"); she will not believe it has already happened until the damage to her body and clothes is pointed out to her. Then her brother is fetched, and she bids farewell to both men in Gospel language: they are to remain firm in their faith and love each other, and not "let our sufferings set a trap for you."

The passage is riddled with gaps. Did Perpetua understand the possibility of walking free when it first arose, though she did not realize yet that she had been charged and hurt by an animal weighing hundreds of pounds? How did she and Felicitas get to the Gate of Life to which they were "called back" or "called over" (the verb is ambiguous), given the blows they have received? Felicitas was unable to get up on her own, and Perpetua is substantially out of her head. Rusticus is said to be with Perpetua only once she reaches the place; he could hardly barge out onto the floor of the amphitheater on his own during the prisoners' ordeals. What did the men say to the women about their choice? Were Christians stringently expected to refuse mercy? Did Perpetua's brother, brought to her only after she has woken up to her bruise or wound, put pressure on her, and if so, in what direction? Was he brought because she was wavering over her choice, or because she was simply in no state to focus on it clearly? Did she forthrightly insist on death with her friends? In any case, her last speech in the text is of a piece with the pious, stilted, biblically tinged language she typically uses to wrap up a passage that shows her vivid and believable individuality:

Fattened for a Sacrifice to Caesar

"Stand fast in your faith, and love one another, all of you, and do not let our sufferings set a trap for you."

Was Perpetua's death in essence a suicide? Could she not bear the thought of leaving most of her contingent—the three men including her trusted friend Saturus—to die without her? Did she confer with Felicitas, or did she make a decision for both herself and the slave woman? Was she made to think—or had she thought so on her own since the beginning—that she would have no life worth living to return to? Had she collapsed psychically from the events of the day, unable to do anything but what she was steered into? Or was she an undistracted, wholehearted Christian, who simply believed that God, already in a loving relationship with her, waited impatiently and without judgment for her company in an eternal realm?

The final scenes in the arena are, I think, also worth quoting in full for easier reference to all their suggestive oddities.

> Also Saturus, who was at another gate, was urging the soldier Pudens by saying this: "So here it is," he said, "just like I knew before and said before: right up to now none of the animals has touched me. So now you can believe with all your heart. Just watch—I'm going ahead, over there, and that leopard's going to finish me off with one bite." Then right away, and at the end of the show, he was thrown to the leopard, and from just one bite blood poured over him, so that as he came back the crowd yelled their taunts at this evidence of a second baptism: "Hope bathing does you good! Hope bathing does you good!" But no doubt about it: the man who had taken a bath this way had done himself a power of good. Then he said to the soldier Pudens, "Goodbye, and keep the faith and me in your mind. And don't let these things upset you: they should do the opposite and set you on firm ground." At the same time, he asked for a ring from the soldier's hand, dipped it in

his own wound, and handed it back to him as a legacy, leaving him a token and memorial of his blood. After that, already unconscious, he was thrown down on the ground with the others to have his throat cut on the usual spot. And after a demand that they be brought to the center of the arena so that, as the sword penetrated their bodies, the audience's eyes could be accomplices to the murder, the group got up on their own and went over to the place where the crowd wanted them. They exchanged kisses, so that they could bring their martyrdom to a perfect conclusion with this ritual of peace. All of them except Perpetua submitted to the blade in stillness and silence, particularly Saturus, who had been the first to ascend the ladder in the vision and was now the first to give up his breath: now too, he was standing by for Perpetua. But Perpetua, in order that she could taste a certain amount of pain, gave a howl as she was stabbed between bones, and then on her own she moved the wavering right hand of the novice gladiator to her throat. Perhaps so great a lady, an object of fear for the unclean spirit, could not have fallen unless she herself had wanted to.[22]

How was the dramatic interaction with Pudens allowed to happen? Could one of the soldiers deployed as guards, animal wranglers, or stage managers converse and transact with a condemned prisoner right on the arena floor, while the violence was ongoing? No part of the events as shown here makes sense. Saturus did not march over to the leopard by his free choice; the condemned were not allowed to arrange their deaths to suit themselves. He was exposed to the animal by force, or perhaps by some prior connivance and the appearance of force. Then, bitten and bleeding profusely without succor, he lost consciousness and was, like anyone *apparently* dead in the arena, brought to the place for throat cutting to ensure that he was dead: it was there that a gladiator's armor would be stripped. But it was an out-of-the-way, ignominious place, and the wrong one in which a Christian martyr should die.

The reaction from the stands (as represented) cuts through this protocol. The prisoners should have been dispatched one by one in prolonged and riveting ways and then had their inert bodies dragged off for the coup de grâce. But according to the narrative, the crowd succumbs at this late moment to an unusually ghoulish impulse: they must *see* the throat cutting. The prisoners cooperate by getting to their feet and walking to the center of the arena — including Saturus, which seems to defy the laws of physiology. But it fits with the literary traditions of martyrdom, and fits even better with martyrdom as this particular group has shaped it, or has been shown shaping it. They must die conspicuously, all together, and with conspicuous dignity.

For all my questions, I hesitate to deny that most of this last scene could have happened as written. For one thing, it was very public as well as climactic and unusual, something people would talk about and remember, making it harder to falsify in literature. For another, the martyrs are young friends, and their relationship with one another has at times crowded against their relationship to anything either abstract or practical. Instead of one of them declaiming about faithfulness, they take this crowning moment to exchange the kiss of peace and line up quietly and neatly for their dispatch, with Perpetua last in line, as if they recognize that she is faltering. If they wanted this exact arrangement for their martyrdom enough, could they not have contrived it somehow — as they somehow contrived a temporary release from jail that included even the two slaves? Maybe they had help from the games' personnel in dying on seemly display together; Christians who had those people's ear could have been their liaisons. And if the spectators were as susceptible as the text claims to events in the arena as a sort of tragic plot, they went home filled with affecting sensations.

Perpetua's special friend Saturus waits for her until she arrives where she needs to go, as on the dream ladder. Again he stands by for her (literally "upholds her") amid the weapons. But how does the narrator know exactly what was going on, let alone any currents between the dying? Saturus was not one of the two stars, Perpetua and Felicitas: the audience at its distance may not even have distinguished him as an individual from the other two men in ordinary clothes.

Perpetua, however, *was* a star, and so her manner of death would have gained more attention and thus been harder to falsify. And I find it highly credible that she behaves less collectedly than those who have tougher backgrounds, and who may have maintained their concentration and composure throughout the horrors of the show. I do not believe that the gladiator (the only one who appears in the *Suffering*), however inexperienced, who was assigned to cut her throat missed it, and jabbed a sword point into her clavicle or ribs. Novice gladiators did cut throats, but this gladiator would have to have been palsied or subnormal to fail at cutting a young woman's throat if there were no interference. What is more, the text indicates that this is the same man who moved down the line, cutting throats one by one, apparently competently. Could he really be another of the professional military men who purportedly quailed before Perpetua?

Perpetua then yelled in terror or pain or both; not, nonsensically, "in order that she could taste a certain amount of pain" — as if yelling were equivalent to hurting, and as if having her throat cut would not hurt enough unless she yelled. She had extra seconds to yell because, emotional and impulsive as she was, she could not keep her hand from pushing the sword away from her neck, and the gladiator had to stab again. If she seized the faltering blade and stabbed herself, like the heroic first-century CE republican rebel Arria, why was she yelling? Or did she, having resisted at first, collect herself and make a move to welcome the blade, the way she would submit to the protocol of bravery and faith after other flights of emotion?

The evident serial smoke-screening is distressing. Perpetua may have been naive, arrogant, stubborn, and egotistical; she may have been obsessed by plans to become the spoiled child of an already exclusive heaven. But she died for the right to be herself: to be with her own chosen friends and mentors; to espouse rare thoughts and purposes and vindicate them in public, to dream wildly and extravagantly; to get into a lot of trouble and stay there. Her story may be contrived, awkward, sometimes farcical, because it is brand new. I call her the twenty-first-century woman's remote ancestor; she deserves to be appreciated in her splendid humanity.

CHAPTER SIX

A Picture with the Face Torn Out

The story of Perpetua must have been epochal in its popularity. The existence of four early, anonymously sourced versions — *The Suffering of the Holy Perpetua and Felicitas*, its Greek translation, and the *Acts of Perpetua and Felicitas* (in two versions) — may not seem unusual to us, but most of the martyrdoms that later became iconic had little or no surviving documentation near the time of the events. Perpetua seems to have caught the imagination in ways no other martyr did.

Her affinity with legendary heroines played some part in this. She presented herself, and was presented, as a woman warrior — a fascinating figure to the ancients — like Hippolyta and Camilla. She was also a helpless noble victim like Andromeda and Psyche, each rescued by a superhuman being. And her female body was a willing sacrifice to a cause, like Lucretia's to marital chastity and Mary's to the incarnation of Jesus. But I think that none of these mythic elements was as powerful for propagating her story as Perpetua's reality, her grounded life and personality. There had never been a woman like this in literature. Women remained to a great extent unacknowledged by men, themselves, and each other; their individual, spontaneous, and inconvenient thoughts were almost absent in the common, lasting discourse that validates personal experience as genuine and worthy of attention. Reading the *Suffering* and its close Greek translation, the most lifelike versions of the story, may have been like listening at a door that had been bolted shut for millennia.

But these versions were not destined to prevail and influence other literature; they had the wrong milieu for that. Early Christianity was distinctly less friendly to interest in people's awkward differences from one another than pagan Greek and Roman culture was.

Perhaps the visual arts show this best. The ancestral portrait busts that aristocratic Romans displayed in their houses started as death masks and kept a commitment to truth through the age of marble: most of these images show tired, mean old men, inflated or dried up by their own authority, their disillusioned eyes set deep in wrinkles or humps of bone. The gods whom Homer says had no sorrows are smooth-faced and eternally serene as statues and wall paintings. Mortals are imprinted with their lives.

During Late Antiquity, Christians were not alone in making the face a mere paradigm — the oval shape, the large eyes, the straight nose, the bland mouth — but this mode did particularly suit the religion, and in time Christ, the Virgin Mary, a saint, or a sovereign would have almost the same inexpressive features. Perpetua herself appears in just this mode in several early images, as a serene noble lady, her perfect hair creating a perfect frame for her visage. She does not look like someone who fell out with her father, spent time in prison, was whipped across an arena, and had a cow sicced on her. Pictorial accuracy would have asserted her humanity, and humanity was a fleshy sack of temptations or the husk for salvation to throw away. During the eighth and ninth centuries in the Byzantine Em-

A Picture with the Face Torn Out

pire the prejudice against earthly being went even farther, and with the sanction of Hebrew Bible prohibitions on figural imagery, holy images themselves were mutilated or destroyed by the iconoclasts: a quick way to purify an icon was to chisel off the face.

On a literary plane, the memory of Perpetua went through both these stages, the washing out of her character and her virtual disappearance as an individual. She had made too much of an impression for her story to be discarded altogether. She and Felicitas inspired a vigorous martyr cult, the kind the church could not hope to suppress and so co-opted. Martyrs' yearly feast days (hers is March 7), celebrating their death and rebirth into eternal life, became official church observances; martyrs were also exploited to illustrate developing Christian theology. But a singular thing about Perpetua among all the remembered martyrs is the enormous gap between what early interpreters could know about her directly, as fact, and the purposes to which they applied it.

Her story of the last days of her life is highly personal, and told without doctrinal ambition. She does not moralize or generalize; she concentrates on her own actions and reactions, thoughts and emotions. Her male companions reportedly threatened a high Roman official with Judgment Day. Perpetua never manifests any interest in the different fates of souls except in a case where she can personally intervene, her dead brother's; her references to the devil and to God are brief and colorless.

Yet a few years after her death, Tertullian used Perpetua as a theological prop. He apparently mixed up her vision of the Good Shepherd's heavenly pasture with Saturus's vision of heaven, and he erroneously argues that only martyrs go directly to heaven because she, the most powerful of martyrs, saw only martyrs there.[1] (Saturus reports seeing individual martyrs he knows, but also "elders" or "old men/people," avatars of two people not yet dead, and distinct "brothers" together with martyrs.)² This is Tertullian's only mention of Perpetua, despite his preoccupation with women and their role in Christianity. Perhaps this woman, a local heroine who was freewheeling in her Christian witness, could fit into his purposes only as a distorted fragment.

I have already mentioned two later versions of Perpetua's story, the *Acts of Perpetua and Felicitas* (*Acta A* and *Acta B*). Some early writers on martyrdom use the Latin word *acta* — in their context, it means "transcripts" — the way pagan historians use the word *annales*, official annual records of important events, to allude to documentary authority. But though judicial proceedings dominate the *Acts* narratives, there is no reason to believe the author or authors did archival research; rather, they seem to have drawn on the *Suffering* but imposed on it many conventional tropes of martyrdom. A lot of that account's wording remains, but its distinctiveness is less in evidence. Perpetua's special voice or writing is gone, although in *Acta A* she is presented telling of her ladder vision in the first person.

She is also demoted from her position as the de facto leader and star of the group, and leeched of her cheekiness. In *Acta A*, Saturus speaks to the governor for all the martyrs after their arrest. Perpetua faces off with her father over her Christianity, but she does not link him with the devil in his campaign of dissuasion or claim to have enjoyed being rid of him. He attacks her, going for her eyes, but then for no apparent reason he leaves the scene "shouting and overcome." There is nothing about the prison conditions or Perpetua's particular anguish or anxiety, only the martyrs' "praying together without ceasing." No one invites her dream of the bronze ladder, and in the dream she shares the attention in heaven with Saturus.³ Perpetua's second vision (there is none concerning her dead brother), of the fight with the Egyptian, is cut far down, and the whole group of martyrs subdues him.

A Picture with the Face Torn Out

Saturus takes the lead as the spokesman in the final hearing, again speaking for everyone, though individual interrogations follow. The governor separates the women from the men and questions Felicitas about her marriage, which she repudiates. (She is not a slave here but a married plebeian, which renders her pregnancy proper.) Perpetua has a long, declamatory face-off with her family at the hearing and throws off her baby, whom her father tries to make her hold. Perpetua's husband, suspiciously absent from the *Suffering*, is present here. The group of her relatives presents a united front, whereas the evidence of the *Suffering* tilts toward her husband no longer being in contact with her or any of the others.

The arena scene is very short, showing only that the martyrs were sent to the beasts naked with their hands tied behind their backs, and indicating how each one died. Saturus and Perpetua are devoured by lions in a single clause, and the other animals are also shown in the plural; no cut-rate, one-per-species feeble attackers here.

Acta B is quite similar, though one difference is of particular interest, as it contains a falsification that will prove critical. The *Suffering*, even with all its bald omissions, cannot hide that the women martyrs suffered and prevailed as women. *Acta B* sweeps away the women's real, chosen, agonizing sacrifices as mothers, as well as any notion that there might be a particular divine mercy for them, one that will allow them to go to heaven without having made their most innocent loved ones victims of their martyrdom. The new version of the story makes the denial of Felicitas's biology its crescendo:

> But because they were in sad sympathy with Felicitas, seeing that she was carrying a burden in her womb for the eighth [we would count this as the seventh] month, they decided to pour out prayers to God for her. And while they held out in prayer, she gave birth.

> Therefore, as Caesar's birthday was on the horizon, the order was given by the governor for them to be led out of the jail. Then with the holy martyrs marching ahead, Felicitas followed, who from desire for Christ and passion for martyrdom had not sought out a midwife, yet felt no injury from the birth; instead, truly happy and about to be made holy by her own blood, she set an example not only to her sex but to manly bravery as well, and was going to seize the crown of martyrdom after the burden of her womb.[4]

Here Felicitas, not Perpetua, is the star, with other martyrs preceding her like an entourage. The *Suffering* shows Felicitas's entry into the arena as triumphant too, but in that telling hers has been a real and natural ordeal that prepares her for the ordeals of the arena: she goes "from blood to blood," from the midwife (implying that she needed and had one) to the gladiator whose weapon is a net, and a second baptism (in blood) will follow her washing after birth. The Latin wording and the syntactical shape of the two passages are similar, both using, among other elements, the future participle. It seems that this author knew the original but went out of his way to deny childbirth and motherhood as legitimate and difficult missions for Christian women, or even as acceptable sacrifices to a more exalted mission. Women's special roles and their most precious results are magicked away as a mere "burden." There is no word about what happened to Felicitas's baby, as a reassurance for womanly or merely human compassion. Erotic desire, the impetus for making babies, is transferred to Christ and self-sacrificial death, as a mere metaphor. Granted, this is more respectful than the *Suffering*'s tart-sounding characterization of Perpetua as a spoiled darling, but not much more respectful.

Around the end of the fourth century, Augustine made Perpetua and Felicitas the topic of three sermons on their feast day, March 7.

A Picture with the Face Torn Out

But martyrdom as such was far from his point. By his time, state sponsorship of the mainstream Christian church—of which Augustine, as bishop of Hippo, was an unrivaled champion—placed it in a position to persecute religious dissenters itself (though execution remained for a long time extremely rare and did not take place in arena games, an institution that Christians continued to denounce). Moreover, Augustine's main Christian rivals during his clerical career were the Donatists, otherworldly purist believers in the strain of the Montanists; Donatists still *did* aspire to martyrdom.

As a celebrated preacher, energetic church leader, ambitious theologian, and fierce controversialist, Augustine wanted above all for people to listen to him without distractions. He thus had his hands full with a personality like Perpetua's. (He cites unique parts of the *Suffering*, establishing that he used this text as a source.) Whereas she tells of martyrdom as an adventure like no other, painful yet glorious, sad yet triumphant, through which her special qualities led her to a sort of super-martyrdom, Augustine uses her as an example of submissive faith: the extremes of her achievements teach what ordinary humans like those in his audience can achieve if they let God act through them.

For Augustine, a blessed afterlife is nothing like what Perpetua looks forward to in her visions: a heaven of physical beauty, friendship, and play, where the brave young winners of the supreme prize are cherished like children and even fed sweets. Augustine's heaven offers no specifically earthly delights, and entails a transcendent reembodiment and an equivalence to angels.[5] Here Perpetua would not get what she wants: there would be nothing left of her with which to want or to be satisfied.

But Augustine is above all uncomfortable with the reality of two women as heroes of his religion. They had caught the popular imagination; this is why the feast day was theirs. But they could not have had a squirmier celebrant than the Bishop of Hippo. Augustine had had such a traumatic experience with sex—a powerful erotic drive; a short period of deeply regretted wild oats, including same-sex experimentation; a long-term mistress he guiltily loved and agonizingly sent away; a son by her who died a few years later—that he eventually laid down the law that the human sexual response was at the root of sin, suffering, and estrangement from God. His Rule for the first monastic order set up within the Catholic church, the Augustinians, spends an inordinate amount of text on the dangers of looking at, speaking to, and thinking about women. What was he going to do rhetorically with women like Felicitas and Perpetua, sexual beings who had been not only vibrant, appealing, and assertive witnesses to their faith in their own right (like his mother, with whom he was uncomfortably close, and whom he restlessly resisted) but also chaste, loyal—though upstaging—companions of the men with whom they died? He shrinks from all these realities and denies, in the face of all the *Suffering*'s evidence, that the women acted, or could have acted, as women.

Augustine emphasizes that they overcame the weakness of their sex to achieve *virtus,* courage, or literally "manliness": thus the miraculous oxymoron of their achievement.

> The result is that even in those who are physically women, manliness of the mind can hide away the sex of the body; and it would be disgusting to think about that thing in the body which could not be evident in their actions. Therefore, the head of the snake was stamped on by an untainted foot and a victorious sole, when the erected ladder was the lesson, the ladder by which the blessed Perpetua could go to God. Thus the head of the primordial serpent, which caused woman's headlong fall, became a step for her as she climbed.[6]

A Picture with the Face Torn Out

Further, Perpetua and Felicitas were not only ladies or generic females (*feminae*) but functional women (*mulieres*); the devil thought they were easy prey, as mothers who were naturally weak through their attachment to their infants; it thus took a greater miracle to infuse them with the masculine manliness (*virilis virtus*) they needed to fight. This is why their names, rather than those of the men, the very strong men who also conquered on that day, are attached to the celebration.[7]

Whenever a dire difficulty in the *Suffering* confronts Augustine, he fudges. Perpetua does not break the commandment to honor her father; her cold, superior, and unavoidably disobedient behavior passes with the bishop for "moderate": in other words, she walked the tightrope the devil has strung for her.[8] How Augustine would have judged a young woman in his own flock who stood out against ungodly behavior by her father boggles the mind by contrast. He approved his mother's submission to a foul-tempered, adulterous pagan husband, and admiringly memorialized her advice to other wives that they had no business complaining about their beatings because the marriage contracts their fathers had signed made them slaves.[9] He evidently had in Perpetua a daunting figure to press into doctrinal service.

Whereas Perpetua's style is quirky, earthy, and vivid, Augustine fires up conventional rhetoric as an engine of dehumanization, chuffing away to make rigid ideology out of experience. Again and again, he puns on *perpetua felicitas,* the eternal blessedness of the two women martyrs, reducing these unusual but quite different women to a single handy abstraction and a figure of speech.

Sometime between Late Antiquity and the High Middle Ages, the impression of Perpetua could become fixed and minimal, like the stereotyped images of holy beings in churches of the time. Traditional stories tend to undergo major changes in structure and presentation in different eras. The story of Spartacus, for example, shifts from the ancient Roman stress on the effectiveness of a general (Crassus) in putting down an anarchic uprising to the broken chains that exemplify modern political liberation to a celebration of homosexual eroticism and solidarity. But in the Early Middle Ages, many interpretive resources and much transformative literary energy were lost. Some of the martyrologies (compendia of accounts of martyrdom) do little or nothing more than record who died on which day of the year, and garbling was an evident risk of greater length. Perpetua's story suffers in both these ways.

Among later, more elaborate versions of the story is one from the thirteenth century, in the *Legenda Aurea* (literally, "golden things to be read," misleadingly called in English the *Golden Legend*), a collection of martyr tales by Jacobus de Voragine. Treatment of Perpetua in the *Legenda* reaches a new degree of blandness and a greater than ever susceptibility to clichés. In the large anthology, Perpetua and Felicitas fall under the heading of Saint Saturninus of Carthage, and her only personal quality explicitly singled out is her noble lineage. In other respects as well, she is like a fairy-tale princess. Her ladder to heaven is not bronze, like a weapon; it is gold, like a trinket. The wrenching problem of her baby's fate after her death has disappeared. Climactically, she is instead confronted with the claim that her husband will not be able to live without her; that is, he will perish from the loss of his beloved. This threat seems more germane to romantic tales than to religious literature; it greatly trivializes the real Perpetua's situation, as far as this was manifest in the *Suffering*.[10]

A complete Latin version of the *Suffering* was discovered in the seventeenth century and an edition of it published in modern book form in 1663. Since then, explication of the text and the context has

A Picture with the Face Torn Out

of course been extensively updated. But whether chiefly because of Perpetua's sex, her complex presence on the page, or religious feeling, she seldom is allowed to appear as anything like her believable self. A special problem for understanding her in the modern era stems from the religious conflicts that did so much to create this era. Too many scholars have insisted that Perpetua *stood for* a Christianity like their own, rather than — as seems obvious to me after a close reading the *Suffering* — that she stomped, stumbled, and gloried her way to death for a cause we cannot picture, which was early in its evolution and quite new to her too; about which she meditated only insofar as it touched her personally; and which she dealt with strictly in the light of her own experience.

The modern bibliography of Perpetua is immense yet mainly scholarly; I at first doubted I could find much to write about that would interest nonspecialist readers. Perpetua is not, after all, a female figure like Sappho or Cleopatra who has ricocheted noisily through a number of subsequent cultures. But then I came across a work of eye-popping exuberance, *The Martyrs of Carthage: A Tale of the Times of Old,* by Mrs. J. B. Webb (also known as Annie Webb-Peploe), a British vicar's wife who gave the world a number of pious historical fictions in the vein of Edward Bulwer-Lytton's *Last Days of Pompeii,* a work of 1834.[11] The 1868 edition of *The Martyrs* is the only one I could access.

Webb includes a preface that superficially resembles that of the redactor of the *Suffering,* setting out the goal of strengthening believers at this late, perilous moment; but her rationale is different from that of the early exponents of Perpetua. Their veracity was not a pressing issue in their own time, because, like everyone else, they worked with few or no good sources: their choice was between copying or adaptively inventing, and authors, of course, adaptively invented. I find some of their views annoying, but they could not have shaped or reshaped these views by means of actual research had they wanted to.

Webb wildly made things up in an era when it was no longer respectable, and when she had no need to; in another outlying middle-class home the young Mary Ann Evans (later George Eliot) studied languages and history on her own and translated a monumental historical-critical work on the Bible, David Strauss's *Life of Jesus, Critically Examined.* Webb was not producing admitted historical fiction, like (if we look far ahead) Amy Peterson's *Perpetua: A Bride, a Martyr, a Passion* (2004) or Malcolm Lyon's *The Bronze Ladder* (2006). Instead, citing works both ancient and modern that had already been shown up as fabricated, and giving no hint of where the seams were between those writers' claims and her own sentimental weavings, she downplays her falsifications and cries up her goal of making people think and feel as they should. She gives no ground to the foundation of rhetoric: to respect the audience and work to bring them around. For leaders of the army of salvation like herself (and like the imperial pacifiers she nods to?), the ends justify the means:

> The principal facts and events which are related in this story are, for the most part, historical: and the trials and sufferings of the Christians are authentic. A few trifling anachronisms have, however, been wilfully committed; and names have been altered, and actions, which really took place, have been attributed to individuals who did not perform them, for the sake of increasing the interest of the narrative. But such liberties appeared quite allowable; as the purpose of the story is to show, generally, the nature and severity of the sufferings to which our Christian brethren in those early ages were subjected, and the spirit in which those sufferings were borne: and thus to excite in our own hearts a deep feeling of gratitude for the blessings of peace and security which

A Picture with the Face Torn Out

have so long been vouchsafed to us; and likewise an earnest resolution to buckle on our *Christian armour,* and be ready for any conflict that may await the Church of Christ in these latter days.[12]

Like *Das Kapital* with its representation of for-profit industrial development as inexorably and cumulatively oppressive, this is a work of the age of propaganda in full swing. The Latin original of the *Suffering* story fills about ten pages of a modern book, and its gaps, equivocations, and other difficulties merit all my tedious chants of "seems," "probably," and "likely." Webb creates a fantasist soap opera that is 443 pages long.

Perpetua's marriage, a blank in the *Suffering,* receives an extensive backstory. Her husband, Marcus, is a brave and energetic Roman soldier, corrupted by idolatry. His deployment in Alexandria for persecutions there allows the author to spread the geography beyond the unedifying region of Carthage (which had nothing but the Scillitan martyrdoms to show for actual Christian history to this point) and allows Webb to bring in the martyrdom of Leonides (misspelled "Leonidas"), the father of Origen.

In her husband's absence, Perpetua is converted to Christianity by the lovely, virtuous, and noble Marcella, whom she meets with parental permission on both sides. The two young women stroll in the country among old Punic ruins like Victorian Anglican tourists exploring the fallen heathen edifices around Rome. Despite her proper coyness in deference to her husband's and parents' views, Perpetua's reason is overcome by such doctrines as the infallibility of the scriptures; her temperament, naturally yielding, yields to God.

A melodramatic blow-up occurs when Marcus returns and confronts Perpetua with her idolatrous duty, but both husband and wife break down in a bout of Dickensian tenderness when their angelic child Elva (evidently a Celtic name connoting brightness), who has also converted, breaks down herself before an instrument of torture and flees to her mother's protective arms: the sentence is commuted to exile, at Marcus's instance. Marcus himself comes around to conversion after the wasting death of his angelic firstborn. Elva, in gentle but hectic tubercular fervor, is happy to expire if it causes her parents to reconcile in Christ. Once both parents are martyred, the matchless Marcella fosters the precious baby son.

To crowd out the obvious commandment-breaking in the story, and the practical incompatibility between Perpetua's call to martyrdom and her wish to honor her father, Webb plays up the tale of Marcella and her father, the martyr Numidicus.

> Marcella could not speak. Tears flowed down her pallid cheeks; and, falling on the helpless form, so lately full of life and vigour, she embraced her beloved father, and kissed his cold brow. Numidicus was the first to speak.
>
> "'Sorrow not for me, as those without hope,' my child," he said. "Ours is but a brief separation; and ere long we shall be united again, to part no more for ever. I go before you to the presence of your Father and my Father, your God and my God. I go to your blessed mother, my sainted Sabina; and all the glorious company of those who have departed in the faith. But, oh! still more: I go to dwell with my Saviour! — with Him who died to purchase for me a place in the many mansions of His Father's house. My child, my darling Marcella, 'be thou faithful unto death, and He will give thee a crown of life!' Promise me this, my love, and I die in perfect peace!"[13]

We are now in the realm of literature that Dickens mocked, the simpering tracts that Evangelicals handed out to the poor in lieu of subsistence wages or food.

Martyrdom has been demonstrably important in the development of religious freedom and other human rights. Martyrs do not have to be the anti-Nazi White Rose underground in thoughtfulness and generosity—they don't even have to be right, according to history's judgment—in order to generate awe for the price they pay for their assertion of meaning against fixed and unlistening authority. It does raise the gorge, then, when their witness is transformed into indoctrinating pap and exploited by that same kind of authority.

The next work on Perpetua I discuss here interests me particularly as a translator, but it has been quite influential in general. I see some of the same word choices and phrasing even in recent translations, commentaries, and monographs, sealing what readers in this generation "know" and feel about Perpetua. This work is W. H. Shewring's English translation of the *Suffering* (with accompanying Latin text), published in 1929 (and in a new edition in 1931). The designer Eric Gill provided Shewring with a new font, the celebrated "Perpetua" (similar to Times New Roman) now found in a standard word-processing array.

The 1931 edition that I examined has been through Vatican censorship and is packaged with Augustine's sermons on Perpetua and Felicitas. Circular arguments like Augustine's, but less modest, adorn the introduction. For example, the church father in a treatise merely noted that the *Suffering* is not canonical (that is, what it says is not mandated guidance to believers) and offered a far-fetched hypothesis for Dinocrates' exit from a purgatory-like realm: he had been baptized but then corrupted by his pagan father; a martyr's prayers can thus help elevate him to heaven after his death. Shewring represents the baptism as definite and makes the first of his blackboarded assertions depend on it:

> (1) S. Perpetua's vision of her brother in Purgatory and of his release through her intercession has particular importance as a very early

testimony to the Church's doctrine on the subject. As S. Augustine explains (*De Anima* I.10), the boy was no doubt a Christian, but was old enough to have committed a venial sin after his baptism.[14]

Assertion 2 is that Perpetua was brought to the Gate of Life not because of an offer to spare her life and that of Felicitas (an offer Perpetua evidently refused while dazed and under the influence of male Christian handlers who were safe themselves) but only for a respite from torment before the execution.[15] I think the text of the *Suffering* and the historic realities of the games speak for themselves on this point.

In assertion 3, Shewring scolds readers who are shocked at the hell-threatening self-righteousness of the male martyrs toward onlookers. "A martyr dies as a witness to the true faith, and it may be his duty towards his enemies to instruct them by his words of the faith which he is to seal with his death." Shewring goes on to claim, as if it were fact, that the words of Saturus at the banquet worked to bring about many conversions.[16] Statements of this kind are interlaced with historical facts and stand beside a quite solid account of the manuscript tradition, and so might be brushed off as the author's understandable reverence for a saint (who is actually named in the Mass, as he mentions).[17] After all, how important are introductions to popular nonfiction books? The main text is usually what counts. But here the denaturing of Perpetua is dragged heavily into the modern era. In Shewring's English, there is no distinction between the Latin style of the redactor and that of Perpetua or Saturus, or between it and the briefly quoted speakers whose words in the original are decidedly colloquial. In the translation, they all speak Renaissance Anglo-Saxon Bible-ese. Here is the beginning of Section 4:

A Picture with the Face Torn Out

> Then said my brother to me: Lady my sister, thou art now in high honour, even such that thou mightest ask for a vision; and it should be shown thee whether this be a passion or else a deliverance. And I, as knowing that I conversed with the Lord, for Whose sake I had suffered such things, did promise him, nothing doubting; and I said: To-morrow I will tell thee.[18]

The stilted Vulgar Latin of early Bible translations from the Greek and Hebrew is nothing like either the redactor's conventional orotundity or the colloquialisms of other writers and speakers in the *Suffering* collection—those gaps are rudimentary matters for a translator to attend to. Yet Shewring's style is not even a good forgery of early modern biblical English but more like a composition recited at a Renaissance Faire. The word *passion* for suffering, for example, is very rare in foundational English Bibles, and even if it were a more solid part of the translation tradition, it would still risk confusing the modern ear: we don't ordinarily say "passion" when we mean "suffering"; the notion that Jesus was passionately devoted to being crucified, rather than that he endured agony, lurks at the back of our minds. Moreover, there are far too many pointless flourishes in this passage, too many extra words: "Then said," "even such," "as knowing," "did promise him."

This pompous rendering entails a betrayal of Catholic (and also Protestant) teachings. Even conformist Christian believers are *allowed* to draw back from Perpetua's story when it troubles them, and to approve it in selective ways, just as Augustine did. The pious premise of his sermons about Perpetua and Felicitas, in fact, is the power of God in making two mere human beings—especially weak human beings, women—into his instruments. This message is harder to accept if they do not sound human.

There are many outright inaccuracies in Shewring's translation too, and they have clung like burrs even to scholarly readings, confusing the story outright. The *faux ami* "vexed" for *vexavit* has Perpetua's father annoying rather than attacking her when he goes for her eyes.[19] In her account of her fourth vision, the adjective *masculus* becomes "a man" and not "like a man": Perpetua undergoes a sex change rather than simply being able to wrestle in regulation nudity without her breasts and female genitals being voluntarily displayed in public.[20]

In recent years, interest in Perpetua can detach itself from the old concerns and manifest a determination to see her as a vessel for identity politics: as a woman, an African, or even – on the basis of this above mistranslation – someone with transgender propensities; at times it can seem as if, to some minds, she never existed except as a shadow of grievances and aspirations peculiar to these past few decades.

Jennifer A. Rea and Liz Clarke's graphic novel is called *Perpetua's Journey: Faith, Gender, and Power in the Roman Empire.* The title latches on to the familiar anachronistic theme of Christian idealism as the David facing Rome's brutal and cynical Goliath, though Roman authorities never did repress Christians for being pure and good, and Christians were at pains to deny that they dissented from the Roman regime. But the graphic novel is anachronistic mainly in a different way, showing Perpetua bursting with beauty and physicality – like Xena, Warrior Princess, or Wonder Woman, with hefty breasts sometimes thrust out eye-catchingly (her image on the cover makes her look as if she were wearing one of those pointy mid-twentieth-century bras), skin and hair always glowing as if in a glamor shot. Felicitas, as her sidekick, is much the same. The living Perpetua and her chosen circle sought to transcend the material world, and especially the longings, the bonds, and the joys and risks

A Picture with the Face Torn Out

of the flesh – which happen to weigh more heavily on women than on men. In that sense, they were better feminists than Rea and Clarke.

My biggest disappointment in the reception of Perpetua, however, is simply that she is so little known. Even to Catholics, she tends to be only a name or an image of lions savaging her in the arena; to most others, she is a font in their software. It is high time to move her story into the brighter light she powerfully deserves. Christians, those of other faiths, and the secular might all feel in the early twenty-first century something of what the early Christians felt: that we are approaching the end times and need courage, conviction, and the willingness to sacrifice ourselves in order to save at least some part of our world. For me certainly, Perpetua, who had comparatively little yet gave so much and did her part in changing history against the odds, is a special inspiration.

The Suffering of the
Holy Perpetua and Felicitas

1 1 If ancient demonstrations of faith, which both bear witness to God's grace and accomplish the instructive building up of humankind, were set out in writing in order that, as if the reading of them were like a vivid re-creation of the event, by means of which God can be celebrated and humankind solaced, then why should not new evidence that is equally suitable to either purpose also be set out? 2 In fact, in the same measure, these present things too are one day going to be venerable and highly useful to our posterity, notwithstanding that in their own era of the here and now they are consigned to lesser influence because a reverence for ancient times is taken for granted.[1] 3 But those people who judge the singular power of the singular Holy Spirit according to ages of historical time should take note: whatever events are less has-been should be considered greater in that they *aren't* as old-news, due to the overflowing abundance of grace that has been ordained for the final segments of the world's time.[2] 4 Indeed, "In the last days," says the Master, "I will pour out my Spirit onto everyone alive, and their sons and daughters will speak out; and on my slaves, both men and women, I will pour out my Spirit; and the young men will see visions, and the old men will dream dreams."[3] 5 Therefore even we — who recognize and honor both the original prophecies and the new visions that are pledged in parallel, and count the other powers of the Holy Spirit as instruction for the Church (to which that same Spirit was sent issuing largess to all the people, just as the Master

The *Suffering*

shares it out to individuals)[4] — have no choice but to both set out such things and make them known through reading aloud for the glory of God, so that no one who is weak or despairing about his faith should think that divine grace was a companion only of the ancients, whether it was granted in the form of martyrs or of revelations; since God always accomplishes what he has promised as evidence for those who do not believe and as a favor to those who do.[5] 6 Therefore we too extend the news of what we have heard and touched to you as well, our brothers and little sons, so that both you who were present at the events should have the Master's glory brought back to mind, and those of you who know by hearing should have common cause with the holy martyrs, and through them with our Master Jesus the Anointed, whose splendor and honor will last for endless ages. Amen.[6]

2 1 Some young people under instruction for baptism were arrested: Revocatus and Felicitas his fellow slave, and Saturninus and Secundulus.[7] Another member of the group was Vibia Perpetua, who came from a respectable family, had a gentleman's education, and had entered a proper marriage.[8] 2 She had a mother and father and two brothers, one of whom was also under instruction for baptism, and a baby son she was still nursing. 3 She was around twenty-two years old.[9] She herself laid out a full narrative of her martyrdom and left it to us, and it begins immediately below. It appears as it was written in her own hand, giving her own impressions.

3 1 While we were still with our attendants,[10] (she says), and my father wanted to turn my resolve upside down with his talk and wouldn't leave off trying to bring me down, because he felt so strongly for me, I said, "Father, do you see — just to give an example — that container lying there, a little pitcher or whatever it is?" And he told me, "Yes." 2 And I told him, "It can't be called by any other name than what it is, can it?" And he said, "No." "It's the

The *Suffering*

same way with me. I can't say that I'm anything other than what I am, a Christian." 3 Then my father, reacting to this word, threw himself at me to tear my eyes out, but he only roughed me up, and he went away defeated, along with the arguments the devil had given him. 4 For the next few days when I didn't have my father around, I thanked the Master, and it was heavenly for me that *he* was gone.[11] 5 In this actual interval of a few days, we were baptized. And the Spirit told me that I was to pray for nothing from that water but to hold out against my body's suffering.[12] After a few days, we were taken in at the jail,[13] and I was terrified, because I'd never been anywhere that dark before. 6 Oh, what a hard day! The heat was overwhelming because of the mobs of people there, and the soldiers were shaking us down. On top of all that, while there I was sick with anxiety about my baby. 7 Then Tertius and Pomponius, blessed ministers who were looking after us,[14] arranged by a certain consideration for us to be allowed into a better part of the jail for a few hours so that we could get some relief. 8 Then we all went out of the prison and could do what we wanted for a while. I nursed my baby, who by this time was weak from not eating. I was worried about him, and I spoke to my mother and encouraged my brother, and I entrusted the baby to them. I was wasting away to see how my mother and brother were wasting away for my sake. 9 For many days I suffered through my worry over things like these. But then I obtained permission for my baby to stay in the jail with me. And right away I got my strength back, and my hardship and worries about my baby were taken off my shoulders, and the jail suddenly became a palace for me, so that I preferred to be there rather than anywhere else.

4 1 Then my brother said to me,[15] "Sister, my lady, now you're held in very gracious regard, so much so that you could pray for a vision, and it would be shown to you whether there will be suffer-

The *Suffering*

ing or a furlough." 2 As for me, I knew I spoke with the Master, whose great favors I had experienced, so I confidently made my brother a promise, saying, "Tomorrow I'll report to you what's happened," and I prayed, and this was shown to me.

3 I saw a bronze ladder, amazingly long, and reaching all the way to the sky, but narrow, so that people could go up it only one at a time. And on the sides of the ladder iron gear of all kinds was stuck in.[16] Swords were there, spears, hooks, single-edged swords, and spikes, so that if somebody climbed carelessly or did not keep looking upward, he would be mangled, and his flesh would cling to the gear. 4 And below this ladder a snake was lying, amazingly big, waiting in ambush for climbers and frightening them away from the climb. 5 But Saturus climbed up ahead; he had not been there at the time we were arrested, but afterward he turned himself in voluntarily for our sake, because he had built us up through his teaching. 6 Then he came to the top of the ladder and turned around and said to me, "Perpetua, I'm holding everything up for you — and upholding you;[17] but keep an eye on the snake so that he doesn't bite you." And I said, "In the name of Jesus the Anointed, he won't do nothing to hurt me."[18] 7 And from under the ladder the snake put his head out slowly, as if he were afraid of me; and as if I were putting my foot on the first rung, I stepped on his head, and climbed up. 8 And I saw a garden, huge in size, and in the middle of it I saw a white-haired person, tall, in a shepherd's clothes, milking sheep, and around him were standing many thousands of people dressed in pure white. 9 And he raised his head and looked at me and said to me, "Welcome, child!"[19] And he called me over and, out of the curd from the milk he had obtained, he gave me more or less a mouthful. And I took it in my cupped hands and ate it. And all those who were standing around said, "Amen." 10 And at the sound of their voices I woke up, still tasting something sweet.[20] And I immediately gave

The *Suffering*

an account to my brother, and we understood that suffering was to come, and from then on we had no hope for anything in this world.

5 1 After a few days, a story was making the rounds that we would have a hearing. But then my father suddenly showed up from the city, and he was afflicted and worn out. He climbed up to me to bring me down,[21] saying, 2 "Have pity on me, my daughter, in my white-haired old age; have pity on your father, if you call me 'father' and I've earned it by bringing you up with my own hands to the blooming young womanhood that you enjoy, and if I've favored you over all your brothers: don't force public disgrace on me. 3 Look at your brothers, look at your mother and her sister, your aunt, look at your son, who won't be able to survive your death. 4 Give up this arrogance, or you're going to do away with all of us. None of us will be able to speak up freely if, ya know, anything's done to you."[22] 5 He said these things to me as a father would, out of his laudable affection for me, and he kissed my hands and threw himself at my feet and wept, no longer calling me "daughter" but "my lady."[23] 6 And I grieved for my father's misfortune, because he was the only one in my whole family who wasn't going to be glad about my suffering, and I tried to comfort him, saying, "What God wants will be done on that platform for the accused. Be cognizant that we do not exist under our own power, but that of God." But he was very sorrowful when he left me.

6 1 On another day, when we were having lunch, we were suddenly seized and taken to a hearing, and we arrived at the forum. Right away, the story made the rounds through the area near the forum, and a huge crowd gathered. 2 We climbed up onto the platform. The others were interrogated and gave their testimony. It was my turn next. But my father appeared on the spot with my son, and pulled me from the stand for the accused, saying, "Make the offering. Have pity on your baby." 3 And the procurator Hilarianus,

The *Suffering*

who had taken over the right of the sword from the governor Minucius Timinianus, who was deceased, said, "Spare your father in his white-haired old age, spare the boy who's just a baby. Perform the rite for the welfare of the emperors."[24] 4 But I answered, "I won't do it." Now Hilarianus asked, "Are you a Christian?" And I answered, "I am a Christian." 5 And when my father insisted on trying to bring me down, Hilarianus ordered him thrown headlong, and he was beaten with a rod.[25] And my father's misfortune hurt me, as if I myself had been beaten; I felt anguish for his wretched old age. 6 Then Hilarianus pronounced sentence on us all and condemned us to the wild animals; but we climbed down in high spirits and returned to the jail. 7 Then, because my baby had become used to nursing at my breasts and staying in the jail with me, I sent Pomponius the minister to my father, asking for the baby.[26] But my father was unwilling to give him to me.[27] 8 But, as God willed it, he didn't crave my breasts any longer, and they weren't inflamed, so that I wasn't afflicted with worry over my baby and pain in my breasts.[28]

7 1 After a few days, while we were all praying, suddenly, in the middle of the prayer, a voice came out of me, and I called out the name Dinocrates. And I was stunned, because he had never entered my mind except then, and now I was in anguish remembering what had happened to him. 2 I recognized that at this very time I was worthy and ought to pray for a vision about him too. And I began to say a prayer for him with great feeling, and to moan to God in sorrow. 3 Immediately, on that very night, this was shown to me.

4 I saw Dinocrates coming out of a shadowy place, where there were many people, and he was burning hot and thirsty, with a dirty face and pale skin, and the lesion in his face that he had when he died. 5 This Dinocrates had been my brother in his life of the body, who at seven years old had died horribly of cancer on his face, so

The *Suffering*

that everyone felt his death was abominable. 6 This was why I had prayed for him; but between me and him there was a huge empty space, so that neither of us could get to the other one.[29]

7 Then, in the place where Dinocrates was, was a pool full of water, and it had a rim that was higher than the boy's height; and Dinocrates was stretching up as if he were trying to drink. 8 I was in anguish, because that pool had water in it, and yet because of the rim's height he wasn't going to be able to drink.[30]

9 And I woke up, and I understood that my brother was tormented, and I had confidence that I could help him in his torment. And I prayed for him every day until we went over to the jail attached to the military base; we were going to fight, you see, at the base's games in honor of Geta Caesar's birthday.[31] 10 And I said prayers for him day and night, groaning and weeping to be given what I prayed for.

8 1 But on a day in which we were kept in the stocks, this was shown to me: I saw the place I had seen before, and Dinocrates with a clean body and nice clothes, and wondrously restored. And where the lesion had been, I saw a scar. 2 And as for the pool I'd seen before, the rim was lowered clear down to the level of the boy's navel, and he drew water from the pool without stopping. 3 And on top of the rim was a gold drinking bowl full of water. And Dinocrates went up to it and started drinking from it.[32] But the drinking bowl was never emptied. 4 And when he'd had enough, he went to play joyfully in the water the way very young children do. And I woke up. Then I understood that he had been taken away from punishment.

9 1 Then, after a few days, an adjutant soldier named Pudens, who was in charge of the prison, started to make much of us, understanding that there was great power in us. He admitted a lot of people to us, so that they could inspire us with good feeling and vice versa. 2 But when the day of the games was close, my father

The *Suffering*

came in to see me. He was wasted away with misery, and he started to rip out his beard and let pieces of it fall on the ground, throw himself down on his face and curse all the years he had lived, and use expressions that could have moved every living thing God made. 3 I was pained at his unhappy old age.

10 1 The day before we were to fight, I saw this seeing: Pomponius the minister had come to the gate of the prison and was knocking violently. 2 And I came out to him and opened up to him. He was dressed in a white garment without a belt, and footwear with complicated laces.[33] 3 And he said to me, "Perpetua, we're waiting for you: come." And he held my hand, and we started to walk by rough, winding paths. 4 It took a long time, and we barely made it, gasping for breath, to the amphitheater. He took me to the middle of the arena, and said to me, "Don't be frightened. I'll be here with you, struggling along with you." Then he went away.

5 Then I saw a huge crowd, extremely excited. But since I knew that I was condemned to face wild animals, I was surprised that no animals were sent against me. 6 Instead, an Egyptian, hideous in his appearance, came out along with his helpers to fight with me. But handsome young men came up to me, my own helpers and supporters. 7 I was stripped down and became like a man. And my crew started to rub me down with oil, the way they usually do for an athletic contest. And opposite me I saw the Egyptian rolling in the wrestling sand.[34] 8 And there came out a man of an amazing size, so that he was actually taller than the highest point of the amphitheater. He was dressed without a belt, in purple, with two stripes over the middle of his chest, and in the same kind of footwear, intricately made of gold and silver, and he was carrying a switch, as if he were a trainer of gladiators, and a green branch that had gold apples on it.[35] 9 And he called for silence and said, "This Egyptian, if he defeats her, will kill her with a sword. But if she defeats

The *Suffering*

him, she will receive this branch." 10 Then he withdrew, and the two of us approached each other and started to throw punches. He was trying to catch hold of my feet, but I was kicking him hard in the face. 11 Then I was lifted up into the air and started to kick him so that it seemed I didn't step on the ground at all. But when I saw there was a pause in the action, I put my hands together, interlocked my fingers, and grabbed his head. And he fell face down, and I stamped on his head. 12 Then the crowd started to shout, and my supporters started to sing a holy song, and I went up to the trainer and took the branch. 13 And he kissed me and said to me, "Daughter, peace be with you." And I started to walk in glory toward the Gate of Life, and then I woke up.[36] 14 And I understood that I wasn't going to fight the wild animals but the devil; I knew, however, that I would have the victory. 15 This is what I did up to the day before the games. How the games turned out, however, anyone who cares to can write about that.

11 1 But the blessed Saturus as well set out this vision of his own, and wrote it up himself. 2 We had suffered, he said, and left our physical bodies, and we started to be carried by four angels toward the East, though their hands didn't touch us.[37] 3 But as we went along we weren't on our backs facing up, but as if we were climbing a gentle slope. 4 And when at the start we were freed from the world, we saw an endless light, and I said to Perpetua (since she was at my side), "This is what the Master promised us: we have come into possession of what was promised." 5 And while we were carried by those same four angels, a broad space opened up in front of us, which looked like a sort of garden with rose trees and all kinds of other flowers. 6 In their height, the trees were like cypresses, and their petals fell without stopping. 7 There in the garden were four other angels, shining brighter than the rest. And when they saw us, they greeted us in terms of honor, and they said with great awe to

the rest of the angels, "Here they are — here they are!" and the four angels who were carrying us were filled with awe, and put us down. 8 Then on our own feet we crossed over into the park.[38] 9 There we found Iocundus and Saturninus and Artaxius, who had burned alive in this same persecution, and Quintus, who had passed away as a martyr in prison. And we asked them where the rest were. 10 The angels said to us, "First come, come inside, and greet the Master."[39]

12 1 And we came up to a place, and the walls around this place seemed to be built out of light, and in front of the gate of that place four angels were standing who dressed us in shining white robes as we went in. 2 And we went in, and we heard voices saying all together, without a pause, "Holy, holy, holy!"[40] 3 And we saw sitting in that same place what looked like a person with white hair. It was like snow, but he had a youthful face; we didn't see any feet.[41] 4 On both his right and left side were four old men, and behind him a huge number of other old men were standing. 5 And we went in with wonder and stood in front of the throne, and the four angels lifted us, and we kissed him, and he passed his hand over our faces.[42] 6 And the rest of the old men said, "Let us stand," and we stood and gave each other the sign of peace.[43] Then the old men said to us, "Go and play." 7 And I said to Perpetua, "You have what you want," and she said to me, "Thanks to God that, happy as I was in my mortal body, I'm even happier here now."

13 1 Then we came out and saw in front of the gates Optatus the overseer at the right and Aspasius the elder and teacher at the left.[44] They were glum and standing apart from each other. 2 Now they threw themselves at our feet and said, "Make peace between us, because you've gone out, and you left us like this." 3 And we said to them, "Aren't you our papa, and you an elder — and you want to throw yourselves at *our* feet?"[45] But we were moved, and we embraced them. 4 Then Perpetua began to talk to them in Greek, and we took them aside under a rose tree in the garden. 5 And while we were speaking to them, the angels said to them, "Let them enjoy themselves; if you have any bad feeling between you, forgive each other." 6 Then they goaded the pair, and they said to Optatus, "Get your people in line, because they meet with you as if they were fans coming back from the chariot races and brawling over the different teams." 7 And so it seemed to us as if they wanted to close the gates. 8 Then we began to recognize many brothers there, and even martyrs. We were all fed by an indescribable fragrance that filled us full.[46] Then I woke up, in joy.

14 1 These are the more striking visions of the martyrs themselves, the most blessed Saturus and Perpetua, which they wrote down on their own. 2 As for Secundulus, God called him while the group was still in the prison, for an earlier departure from this world, and this was not without favor, because he would be spared the beasts. 3 Yet his body, although not his soul, knew a sword.[47]

15 1 Concerning Felicitas, however, the favor of God fell to her lot in the following way. 2 Since she was now carrying a eight-month-old fetus (she was pregnant when arrested), as the day of the spectacle loomed, she was in terrible sorrow at the thought that she would be given a reprieve because of the fetus (because it is not lawful for pregnant women to be exhibited for punishment) and pour out her holy and innocent blood later, among wicked criminals.[48] 3 Her fellow martyrs were grievously sad too, in case they should have to leave such a good comrade behind alone, as a lonely traveler on the road to a destination they all hoped for. 4 Therefore they joined all their groaning together and poured out a prayer to the Master two days before the games. 5 Immediately after the prayer, the pains of childbirth seized her. And when she was in agony, laboring with the natural difficulty of giving birth in the eighth month, one of the assistant jailers said to her, "You're in so much pain now—what will

The *Suffering*

you do when you're thrown to the beasts? You didn't think they were worth considering when you refused to make the sacrifice." 6 But she answered him, "Now it's just me, suffering what I'm suffering. But in that place there will be someone else in me who will suffer for me, because I'm going to suffer for him." 7 After this she gave birth to a girl, whom a certain sister brought up as her own daughter.

16 1 Since, then, the Holy Spirit allowed, and by allowing willed, a narrative of the spectacle itself to be written up, although we are unworthy to add anything to an account of such great glory, still, we will carry out what amounts to a testamentary injunction of the most holy Perpetua — or what is in fact her solemn charge, adding one further proof of her stalwartness and the loftiness of her mind.[49] 2 When the tribune was imposing more stringent restrictions on the prisoners than usual, because the warnings of the most empty-headed people had caused him to fear that they would be extracted from the prison by certain magical spells, Perpetua answered him to his face: 3 "Why on earth don't you allow us to enjoy ourselves? We're the most distinguished criminals, we clearly belong to Caesar, and we're going to fight on his birthday. Wouldn't it be to your great credit if we're fatter when we're led out there?" 4 The tribune shuddered and turned red; and after this he ordered them to be treated more humanely, and the result was that her brothers and other people had the opportunity of coming in and enjoying their company — now that even the adjutant who ran the prison was a believer.

17 1 Also, on the day before the spectacle, when they had the final banquet, which they call "for free men," as far as it was in their power the prisoners enjoyed it not as that, but as a love banquet.[50] They taunted the crowd with the same stalwartness, threatening them with the judgment of God, testifying to the happiness of their

The *Suffering*

suffering, and making fun of the nosiness of those who flocked together there. Saturus said, 2 "Tomorrow isn't enough for you? Why are you glad to see what you hate? Today you're friends, tomorrow you're enemies. But take a good look and remember our faces, so that you recognize us on that all-important day."[51] 3 Hearing that, they were shaken to the core and left, and many of them became believers.

18 1 The day of their victory dawned, and they marched out of the prison and into the amphitheater as cheerfully as if they were going to heaven, with dignified expressions on their faces, and if they happened to tremble, it was from joy rather than fear.[52] 2 Perpetua followed with a shining face and a calm gait, as the lawful wife of Christ, as the pampered darling of God, the strength of her gaze causing all the stares to drop; 3 likewise Felicitas, rejoicing that she had survived childbirth in order to fight the beasts, going from blood to blood, from the midwife to the gladiator who fights with a net, about to wash after birth with a second baptism.[53] 4 And when they had been led up to the gate and were being forced to put on costumes, the men to be dressed as priests of Saturn, and the women as consecrated devotees of Ceres, that noble woman fought back stalwartly clear to the end. 5 She in fact said, "We come here of our own will, so that our liberty will not be crushed. That's the reason we have given over our lives: to avoid doing anything like this. This is the contract we have made with you."[54] 6 Injustice recognized justice; the tribune gave in. Just as they were, in their ordinary clothes, they were led in. 7 Perpetua sang a holy song, already stamping on the head of the Egyptian. Revocatus, Saturninus, and Saturus threatened the crowd that watched them. 8 Next, when they came under Hilarianus's stare, they proceeded to convey to him with gestures and movements of their heads: "You condemn us, but God will condemn you." 9 The crowd was aggravated at this

The *Suffering*

and demanded that the prisoners be driven with scourges down the line of hunters; and at any rate they were gratified that they had attained something of the Master's suffering.[55]

19 1 But the one who had said, "Ask, and you will receive," gave those who asked him for it the ending that each craved.[56] 2 Whenever they had discussed among themselves their longing for martyrdom, Saturninus declared that he wanted to be thrown to all kinds of beasts, as presumably he would wear a more glorious victory garland. 3 Therefore, in the first clash of the spectacle, he and Revocatus had the leopard to deal with, and also were attacked by the bear while they were on the stand.[57] 4 Saturus, on the other hand, hated nothing more than a bear, and he was confident that he would be finished off by one bite of the leopard. 5 Therefore, when he was placed at the disposal of a wild boar, the hunter who had tied him to the boar was instead gored by the same beast and died a few days after the games; Saturus was only dragged. 6 Then when he was fastened to the platform for the bear, the bear refused to come out of its cage. Thus Saturus, unhurt, was called back a second time.

20 1 For the girls, however, the devil prepared a monstrously fierce cow; its purchase was contrary to custom but on purpose: he matched it to their sex.[58] 2 Accordingly they were stripped bare and brought out covered only in nets. The crowd shuddered to see the two, one a girl brought up in luxury, and the other fresh from childbirth, with her breasts still dripping milk. 3 Hence they were withdrawn and dressed in unbelted tunics. Perpetua was tossed first, and landed on her backside. 4 Then when she sat up, she pulled her tunic, which had been torn down the side, back over her to cover her thigh, more conscious of modesty than pain. 5 Next she asked for a clip and pinned up her disordered hair: it was not seemly for a female martyr to have disheveled hair while she was suffering, in case she seemed to be mourning when she was actually in her glory.⁵⁹ 6 Then she got up and, when she saw that Felicitas had been slammed down, she went over to her, took her by the hand, and helped her to her feet. Then the two stood side by side. 7 But the hardheartedness of the crowd was overcome, and the two were called back to the Gate of Life.⁶⁰ 8 There Perpetua was taken over by a certain candidate for baptism named Rusticus, who was attached to her. She was roused from a sort of sleep (she was so deep in the spirit and in a trance) and began to look around her, and to the surprise of everyone, said, "When do we get brought out to that cow sort of thing?" 9 And when she was told that this had already happened, she wouldn't believe it until she recognized on her body and clothes certain marks from the tossing. 10 After that, her brother and the above-mentioned candidate for baptism were summoned, and she addressed them, saying, "Stand fast in your faith, and love one another, all of you, and do not let our sufferings set a trap for you."

21 1 Also Saturus, who was at another gate, was urging the soldier Pudens by saying this: "So here it is," he said, "just like I knew before and said before: right up to now none of the animals has touched me. So now you can believe with all your heart. Just watch—I'm going ahead, over there, and that leopard's going to finish me off with one bite." 2 Then right away, and at the end of the show, he was thrown to the leopard, and from just one bite blood poured over him, so that as he came back the crowd yelled their taunts at this evidence of a second baptism: "Hope bathing does you good! Hope bathing does you good!" 3 But no doubt about it: the man who had taken a bath this way had done himself a power of good.⁶¹ 4 Then he said to the soldier Pudens, "Goodbye, and keep the faith and me in your mind. And don't let these things upset you: they should do the opposite and set you on firm ground."⁶² 5 At the same time, he asked for a ring from the soldier's hand, dipped it

The *Suffering*

in his own wound, and handed it back to him as a legacy, leaving him a token and memorial of his blood. 6 After that, already unconscious, he was thrown down on the ground with the others to have his throat cut on the usual spot.[63] 7 And after a demand that they be brought to the center of the arena so that, as the sword penetrated their bodies, the audience's eyes could be accomplices to the murder, the group got up on their own and went over to the place where the crowd wanted them. They exchanged kisses, so that they could bring their martyrdom to a perfect conclusion with this ritual of peace. 8 All of them except Perpetua submitted to the blade in stillness and silence, particularly Saturus, who had been the first to ascend the ladder in the vision and was now the first to give up his breath: now too, he was standing by for Perpetua.[64] 9 But Perpetua, in order that she could taste a certain amount of pain, gave a howl as she was stabbed between bones, and then on her own she moved the wavering right hand of the novice gladiator to her throat.[65] 10 Perhaps so great a lady, an object of fear for the unclean spirit, could not have fallen unless she herself had wanted to.[66]

11 O martyrs, with your supreme bravery and blessedness! O you who were truly called and chosen for the glory of our master Jesus Christ! Whoever exalts and extolls and worships this glory should in particular read of these new inspirations that are no less worthy than the old ones for the teaching and building up of the Church, so that new displays of valor can bear witness that one and the same Holy Spirit is always at work, even up to the present time, along with the all-powerful God the father and his son Jesus Christ, our master, whose splendor and measureless power will last for endless ages. Amen.[67]

Source Notes

All translations of ancient literature, including of Greek and Latin versions of the Bible, that appear in this book are my own.

INTRODUCTION

Perpetua has been a popular figure from the first, inspiring many versions of her story and many more reactions to it. Since this present book is a biography, I concentrate on the Latin work *Passio Sanctarum Perpetuae et Felicitatis*, widely thought to be the earliest account of her martyrdom and to include her own narration. A Greek version is a close translation composed during antiquity, and shows few significant differences from the Latin text. The earliest revised account of the martyrdom is titled in Latin *Acta Perpetuae* (something like *The Proceedings of Perpetua*), and in English the *Acts of Perpetua and Felicitas*. The *Acta* (having both an *A* and a *B* version) originates from an unknown date but is probably at least several decades later than the *Passio;* as a rewrite, I discuss it only in Chapter 6, as the first major evidence of Perpetua's reception.

Modern introductions to Perpetua include William Farina, *Perpetua of Carthage: Portrait of a Third-Century Martyr* (Jefferson, N.C.: McFarland, 2009); Barbara K. Gold, *Perpetua: Athlete of God* (New York: Oxford University Press, 2018); and Jan N. Bremmer and Marco Formisano, eds., *Perpetua's Passions: Multidisciplinary Approaches to the "Passio Perpetuae et Felicitatis"* (New York: Oxford University Press, 2012).

CHAPTER 1. BORN, EDUCATED, MARRIED

A summary of the archaeological evidence concerning Perpetua can be found in William Tabbernee, "Montanism and the Cult of the Martyrs in Roman North Africa: Reassessing the Literary and Epigraphic Evidence," in *Text and the Material World: Essays in Honour of Graeme Clarke*, ed. Elizabeth Minchin and Heather Jackson, Studies in Mediterranean Archeology and Literature 185 (Uppsala: Astrom, 2017), 299–313. The exchange of letters between Pliny and Trajan concerning the treatment of Christians (10.96–97) is translated in Pliny the Younger, *Letters and Panegyricus*, vol. 2: *Books 8–10, Panegyricus*, ed. and trans. Betty Radice, Loeb Classical Library 59 (Cambridge: Harvard University Press, 1969). For the *Letter of the Churches of Vienne and Lyon*, which goes under other titles as well, I have consulted Frederick W. Weidmann's translation of "The Martyrs of Lyon," in *Religions of Late Antiquity in Practice*, ed. Richard Valantasis (Princeton: Princeton University Press, 2018), 398–412. E. C. E. Owen's translations in *Some Authentic Acts of the Early Martyrs* (Oxford: Clarendon, 1927) include both the Lyon letter and the *Acts of the Scillitan Martyrs*.

CHAPTER 2. CONVERGING FORCES

An excellent resource concerning women in antiquity is Mary R. Lefkowitz and Maureen B. Fant, eds. and trans., *Women's Life in Greece and Rome: A Source Book in Translation*, 4th ed. (Baltimore: Johns Hopkins University Press, 2016). A Latin text and a translation of the letter of Pliny (5.16) on the death of Fundanus's daughter can be found in Pliny the Younger, *Letters and Panegyricus*, vol. 1: *Letters, Books 1–7*, ed. and trans. Betty Radice, Loeb Classical Library 55 (Cambridge: Harvard University Press, 1969). The part of Livy's history cited is translated in *The Early History of Rome*, trans. Betty Radice (Harmondsworth, U.K.: Penguin Classics, 1960). The classic work on the rise of Christianity is Robin Lane Fox's *Pagans and Christians* (New York: Knopf, 1987). A study of ancient martyrdom from nontraditional angles is Joyce E. Salisbury's *The Blood of Martyrs: Unintended Consequences of Ancient Violence* (New York: Routledge, 2004). An inquiry into Perpetua's possible affiliation within Christianity can be found in Rex D. Butler, *The New Prophecy and "New Visions": Evidence of Montanism in "The Passion of Perpetua and Felicitas"* (Washington, D.C.: Catholic University of America Press, 2006). I have used Rudolph Arbesmann's translation of Tertullian's "To the Martyrs" in *Disciplinary, Moral, and Ascetical Work*, ed. and trans. Rudolph Arbesmann, Emily Joseph Daly, and Edwin A. Quain (New York: Catholic University of America Press, 1959), 13–29. I have also used Edwin A. Quain's translation of Tertullian's "Flight in Time of Persecution" in the same book, 271–307. A resource for *The Acts of Paul and Thecla* is Leslie K. Hayes, "The Acts of Thecla: Introduction, Translation, and Notes" (Ph.D. diss., Claremont Graduate University, 2016).

CHAPTER 3. HER OWN HAND, HER OWN IMPRESSIONS

An unexpurgated edition of Anne Frank's diary is David Barnouw and Gerrold van der Stroom, eds., *The Diary of Anne Frank: The Revised Critical Edition* (New York: Doubleday, 1989).

CHAPTER 4. I KNEW I SPOKE WITH THE MASTER

Some general background for readers may include James Gollnick, *Dreams in the Psychology of Religion*, Studies in the Psychology of Religion 1 (Lewiston, N.Y.: Edwin Mellen Press, 1987); Kelly Bulkeley, *Visions of the Night: Dreams, Religion, and Psychology* (Albany: State University of New York Press, 1999); and Sigmund Freud, *The Interpretation of Dreams*, trans. Joyce Crick (Oxford: Oxford University Press, 1999).

Source Notes

CHAPTER 5. FATTENED FOR A SACRIFICE TO CAESAR

Among general works on Roman games are Susanna Shadrake, *The World of the Gladiator* (Stroud, U.K.: Tempus, 2005); Jerry Toner, *The Day Commodus Killed a Rhino: Understanding the Roman Games* (Baltimore: Johns Hopkins University Press, 2014); Donald G. Kyle, *Sport and Spectacle in the Ancient World*, 2nd ed. (Malden, Mass.: Blackwell, 2014); Alison Futrell, *The Roman Games: A Sourcebook* (Malden, Mass.: Blackwell, 2006); and Roger Dunkle, *Gladiators: Violence and Spectacle in Ancient Rome* (Harlow, U.K.: Pearson Education, 2008). The exchange of letters between Pliny and Trajan concerning the treatment of Christians is translated in Pliny the Younger, *Letters and Panegyricus*, vol. 2: *Books 8–10, Panegyricus*, ed. and trans. Betty Radice, Loeb Classical Library 59 (Cambridge: Harvard University Press, 1969).

CHAPTER 6. A PICTURE WITH THE FACE TORN OUT

Summary works on the early reception of the Perpetua story include *The Passion of Perpetua and Felicitas in Late Antiquity*, ed. L. Stephanie Cobb, trans. Andrew S Jacobs and L. Stephanie Cobb (Oakland: University of California Press, 2021), which is particularly useful in that it features full translations of the relevant texts through the martyrologies, including Augustine's sermons; and Margaret Cotter-Lynch, *Saint Perpetua Across the Middle Ages: Mother, Gladiator, Saint* (New York: Palgrave Macmillan, 2016). Tertullian's *Treatise on the Soul* is translated by Peter Holmes in *Ante-Nicene Fathers*, vol. 3, ed. Alexander Roberts, James Donaldson, and A. Cleveland Coxe (Buffalo, N.Y.: Christian Literature, 1885). Nothing on earth compares to Mrs. J. B. Webb's *The Martyrs of Carthage: "A Tale of the Times of Old,"* rev. ed. (London: Richard Bentley, 1868). The translation of the *Suffering* I discuss is Walter Shewring, *The Passion of SS. Perpetua and Felicity, MM: A New Edition and Translation of the Latin Text, Together with the Sermons of St. Augustine upon These Saints, Now First Translated into English* (London: Sheed and Ward, 1931). The graphic novel I cite is Jennifer A. Rea and Liz Clarke, *Perpetua's Journey: Faith, Gender, and Power in the Roman Empire* (New York: Oxford University Press: 2018).

THE SUFFERING OF THE HOLY PERPETUA AND FELICITAS

As an aid to my translation, I began with James W. Halporn, *Passio Sanctarum Perpetuae et Felicitatis* (Bryn Mawr, Pa.: Bryn Mawr Latin Commentaries, 1984), a Latin text with basic commentary. For more complicated interpretive matters, my starting point was Thomas J. Heffernan, *The Passion of Perpetua and Felicity* (New York: Oxford University Press, 2012), which offers extensive supplementary material, including an English translation of the Latin text and an exhaustive, multidisciplinary commentary.

Notes

INTRODUCTION

1. The title in Latin is *Passio sanctarum Perpetuae et Felicitatis*. I have adopted "suffering" as a translation of *passio*, in place of the traditional "passion," which can be misleading to modern readers of English. *Sanctarum*, "holy," is usually translated as "Saints," but to use that word would be to heap anachronistic notions on the "holy ones" of early Christianity.

2. *The Suffering of the Holy Perpetua and Felicitas* 2.3 (hereafter *Suffering*).

3. The Montanist movement started in an area of Asia Minor that had a distinct Eastern culture, and the movement was at least initially open to women's leadership. Adherents appear to have preached continuing revelation, as opposed to scripture-based teachings handed down from an established church hierarchy.

4. See William Farina, *Perpetua of Carthage: Portrait of a Third-Century Martyr* (Jefferson, N.C.: McFarland, 2009), 12–13.

5. *Suffering* 18.2.

CHAPTER 1. BORN, EDUCATED, MARRIED

1. *Suffering* 2.1–3.

2. See, e.g., Augustine, *Sermons* 280–282, available in *The Passion of Perpetua and Felicitas in Late Antiquity,* ed. L. Stephanie Cobb, trans. Andrew S. Jacobs and L. Stephanie Cobb (Oakland: University of California Press, 2021).

3. See Acts 8:27–39 for the story of Philip and the Ethiopian.

4. *Suffering* 8.3.

5. Ibid., 13.4

6. Ibid., 5.2, 2.2.

7. Ibid., 6.5.

8. Ibid, 5.4.

9. Ibid., 3.8.

10. See 1 Corinthians 13:10–15.

11. *Suffering* 2.1.

12. Ibid., 3.1–2.

13. Ibid., 5.6.

CHAPTER 2. CONVERGING FORCES

1. Juvenal, *Satires* 6.161–183, translation available in Juvenal, *The Sixteen Satires*, trans. Peter Green (London: Penguin Classics, 1999).

2. *Suffering* 5.2.

3. Pliny the Younger, *Letters* 5.16.

4. Juvenal, *Satires* 6.398–412.

5. Livy, *From the Founding of the City* 1.57, translation available in *The Early History of Rome*, trans. Betty Radice (Harmondsworth, U.K.: Penguin Classics, 1960).

6. *Suffering* 1.4.

7. See 1 Timothy 2:15, 5:13.

8. *Suffering* 11.9, 13.8.

9. Ibid., 4.

10. See 1 Corinthians 7:28–34.

11. On the rights of fiancés, see 1 Corinthians 7:36–38: a Christian man needs to decide whether or not to marry "his" virgin.

12. *Suffering* 3.1–5, 5.6.

13. Ibid., 5.1–5.

14. Ibid., 3.7–8, 8.1.

15. Ibid., 3.6–8. I have translated 3.8 "weak from not eating" in *The Suffering*.

16. Ibid., 3.9.

17. Ibid., 3.5–7.

18. Ibid., 15.5.

19. *Letter from Vienne and Lyon* 1.27, available in Frederick Weidmann's translation in *Religions of Late Antiquity in Practice*, ed. Richard Valantasis (Princeton: Princeton University Press, 2018), 398–412.

20. *Suffering* 6.

21. Ibid., 9.

22. Ibid., 7–8.

23. Ibid., 20.2–3.

24. Ibid., 3.5–6.

25. Ibid., 7–8.

26. Ibid., 20:1–3.

CHAPTER 3. HER OWN HAND, HER OWN IMPRESSIONS

1. *Suffering* 3.5–8.

2. Longinus, *On the Sublime* 10, available in Aristotle, Longinus, Demetrius, *Poetics, On the Sublime, On Style*, trans. Stephen Halliwell, W. Hamilton Fyfe, Doreen C. Innes, W. Rhys Roberts, rev. Donald A. Russell, Loeb Classical Library 199 (Cambridge: Harvard University Press, 1995).

3. For Jesus, see Luke 4:16–21; for Paul, 1 Corinthians 14.

4. See 1 Corinthians 15:12–55.

5. See 1 Corinthians 14:35.

6. Tertullian, *Flight in Time of Persecution* 6, available in a translation by Edwin A. Quain, in *Disciplinary, Moral, and Ascetical Work*, ed. and trans. Rudolph Arbesmann, Emily Joseph Daly, and Edwin A. Quain (New York: Catholic University of America Press, 1959), 271–307. For Jesus's command to his disciples, see Matthew 10:23.

7. This saying is adapted from Acts 2:17–18, which adapts it from Joel 2:28.

8. *Suffering* 1.4–5.

9. Ibid., 3.1–5.

10. Ibid., 2.3.

11. Ibid., 7.1–2, 7.10.

12. Ibid., 6.5.

13. Ibid., 6.7–8.

14. Ibid., 8.1.

15. Ibid., 20.2.

16. Ibid., 5.6.

17. Ibid., 16.2–4.

18. Ibid., 18.4–6.

19. Ibid., 17.2.

20. Ibid., 11–13.

21. Ibid., 11.2.

22. Ibid., 12.5–6.

23. Ibid., 11.8.

24. Ibid., 11.9.

25. Ibid., 11.7.

26. Ibid., 12.1.

27. Ibid., 11.6.

CHAPTER 4. I KNEW I SPOKE WITH THE MASTER

1. *Suffering* 4.1.

2. See Matthew 17:1–8, Luke 9:28–36 (Jesus on the mountain); 2 Corinthians 12:1–7 (Paul's vision).

3. *Suffering* 4.10.

4. Ibid., 4.5.

5. Ibid., 11–13.

6. Genesis 3:15.

7. See Revelation 1.14.

8. *Suffering* 20.10.

9. Ibid., 9.

10. Ibid., 7.10.

11. Ibid., 10.1.

12. Ibid., 3.7, 6.7.

13. Revelation 3:18–21.

14. *Suffering* 12.5.

15. *The Shepherd of Hermas* 1.3, available in *The Apostolic Fathers,* vol. 2: *Epistle of Barnabas. Papias and Quadratus. Epistle to Diognetus. The Shepherd of Hermas,* ed. and trans. Bart D. Ehrman, Loeb Classical Library 25 (Cambridge: Harvard University Press, 2003).

16. See Revelation 11.8; Tertullian, *Against Marcion* 3.13.10.

17. *Suffering* 19.

18. Ibid., 17.2, 18.7–8.

19. Ibid., 11.5, 11.7–8, 11.10.

20. Ibid., 12.2–7.

21. Ibid., 13.5–7.

CHAPTER 5. FATTENED FOR A SACRIFICE TO CAESAR

1. Petronius, *Satyricon* 45, available in translation by Sarah Ruden (Indianapolis: Hackett, 2000).

2. Apuleius, *The Golden Ass* 4.13–14, available in translation by Sarah Ruden (New Haven: Yale University Press, 2011).

3. *Suffering* 19.6.

4. Petronius, *Satyricon* 45.

5. *Suffering* 15.5; 20.1–3.

6. Ibid., 6.3–5.

7. Tertullian, *Apology* 50, available in translation in Tertullian, Minucius Felix, *Apology, De Spectaculis, Octavius*, trans. T. R. Glover and Gerald H. Rendall, Loeb Classical Library 250 (Cambridge: Harvard University Press, 1931).

8. *Suffering*, 7.9.

9. Ibid., 21.7.

10. Juvenal, *Satires* 6.347–348, available in Juvenal, *The Sixteen Satires*, trans. Peter Green (London: Penguin Classics, 1999).

11. *Suffering* 3.5–6.

12. Ibid., 3.7–8.

13. Ibid., 6.1.

14. Ibid., 9.1.

15. Ibid., 16.2–4.

16. Ibid., 16.3–4, 18.4–5.

17. Ibid., 18.2.

18. Ibid., 18.3.

19. Ibid., 18.4–6.

20. Ibid., 18.7–9.

21. Ibid., 20.3–10.

22. Ibid., 21.1–9.

CHAPTER 6. A PICTURE WITH THE FACE TORN OUT

1. Tertullian, *On the Soul* 55.4.

2. *Suffering* 11.9, 12.4, 13.1–5, 13.8.

3. *Acta A* 3, in *Acts of Perpetua and Felicitas*. Translations of both *Acta A* and *B* available in *The Passion of Perpetua and Felicitas in Late Antiquity*, ed. L. Stephanie Cobb, trans. Andrew S. Jacobs and L. Stephanie Cobb (Oakland: University of California Press, 2021).

4. *Acta B* 8.1–9.2, in *Acts of Perpetua and Felicitas*.

5. See *Suffering* 4.9–10; Augustine, *Sermons* 280.5.

6. Augustine, *Sermons* 280.1.

7. Ibid., 282.2–3.

8. Ibid., 281.2.

9. Augustine, *Confessions* 9.19.

10. *Legenda Aurea* 173, available in translation in Jacobus do Voragine, *The Golden Legend: Readings on the Saints*, trans. William Granger Ryan (Princeton: Princeton University Press, 2012).

11. Bulwer-Lytton is best known today for a single sentence, "It was a dark and stormy night," and for inspiring a yearly competition in awful writing, with winners like Steven Garman of Pensacola, Florida, whose entry concludes, "Flick your Bic, crisp that chick, and you'll feel my steel through your last meal."

12. Mrs. J. B. Webb, *The Martyrs of Carthage: "A Tale of the Times of Old,"* rev. ed. (London: Richard Bentley, 1868), iii–iv

13. Ibid., 169.

14. Walter Shewring, *The Passion of SS. Perpetua and Felicity, MM* (London: Sheed and Ward, 1931), xv.

15. Ibid.

16. Ibid., xv–xvii.

17. Ibid., xviii.

18. Ibid., 25.

19. Ibid., 24; *Suffering* 3.3.

20. Shewring, *Passion,* 31; *Suffering* 10.7.

THE SUFFERING OF THE HOLY PERPETUA AND FELICITAS

1. These are views associated with the New Prophesy or Montanist movement of Christianity, which preached continuing revelation that could be equal in authority to established scripture.

2. In Latin, the play on two slangy-sounding late Latin words, *novitiora* (less has-been) and *novissimiora* (aren't as old-news), may refer to Jesus's repeated witty scolding of his followers: they are hopelessly out of date in looking to the ancient Jewish law for guidance.

3. Adapted from Acts 2:17–18, which adapts Joel 2:28–29.

4. The word "largess" (Latin *donativa*) is used for the bonus that might be given to each soldier in the Roman army on a public occasion.

5. See Romans 4:21.

6. See 1 John 1:1–3.

7. "Fellow slave" can mean the wife of a slave. Perpetua is the only Christian identified here by more than a single name, a distinction probably meant to designate her as a member of the ancestral citizen class.

8. She was married "in the manner of a matron," which points to the highest class of wives.

9. By modern reckoning, she would be around twenty-one.

10. "Attendants" (*prosecutores* in Latin) is a more respectful term than "guards," indicating that the group was under some form of house arrest.

11. "Heavenly for me": literally, "I cooled off."

12. This is a reference to the water of baptism; once baptized, a believer was encouraged to treat the Holy Spirit as an inward guide, especially in the important first prayer after emerging.

13. Probably the main citadel jail in the city of Carthage.

14. The *diaconi* (the word derives from a Greek one for a religious attendant or official) were the Christian functionaries working under the *episcopus* (overseer), the head of the community. "Bishop" and "deacon" are anachronistic terms.

15. "My brother" is either Perpetua's biological brother or a brother in the faith.

16. The vision reflects Jacob's dream of a ladder to heaven in Genesis 28, but the metal hazards and the snake are additions by Perpetua.

17. Saturus makes a pun on the word *sustineo,* which means both "wait for" and "hold up."

18. I have used nonstandard English to mark one of Perpetua's more obvious de-

viations from the grammar of Classical Latin: the verb *noceo* (hurt) takes an indirect object according to the Classical rules that still applied to formal usage, but she uses a direct object.

19. Jesus's word for "child" is Greek, *teknon*.

20. In the early church, a ritual milk-and-honey drink followed baptism.

21. There might be a play on words here, as the father climbs up to the physically lofty citadel prison literally to "bring down" the daughter, an expression that means to make her act against her faith, as in 3.1 and 6.5.

22. The word "free" and its derivatives suggest ancient rights of citizenship. With "ya know," I substitute some slang for an untranslatable deviation from the rules of Classical Latin grammar.

23. *Domina* (my lady) is the word a slave would use.

24. A procurator could fill in for a proconsul or governor, with rights that extended to capital punishment. Septimius Severus was emperor, and had declared his older son Caracalla co-ruler in the year 198.

25. A number of rods tied around an ax handle and carried by a magistrate's attendant symbolized the right of corporal and capital punishment. But it was unlawful to inflict a degrading punishment like this on a citizen.

26. Pomponius is the *diaconus* mentioned at 3.7.

27. Legally and customarily, Perpetua's husband or his family should have custody of the baby.

28. The father's and God's will are contrasted by a pointed rhyme: *noluit* (didn't want) and *voluit* (wanted).

29. For "empty space" she uses *diastema*, a Greek word.

30. The water symbolizes the baptism that Dinocrates missed by dying young. He is thus trapped in an early version of purgatory.

31. Geta was the emperor Septimius Severus's younger son and future co-ruler; his fourteenth birthday—perhaps the occasion for his coming-of-age ceremonies—would have been an apt occasion for celebratory games. It would date Perpetua's martyrdom precisely to March 7, 203. The location of the martyrs' death at a military base is much more problematic, as there was no large base near Carthage.

32. For "cup," there is another Greek word, *fiala*, which appears repeatedly in Revelation.

33. Long loose robes were worn for certain pagan rites. White was the special color of martyrdom, signifying that Christ's blood had paradoxically washed the garments spotless. This is the first known instance of the word *galliculae* for shoes.

34. Perpetua uses the Greek word, *agon*, for the contest, and a technical Greek word, *afa*, for the wrestling sand.

35. In addition to the fancy shoes, this figure is dressed in clothing that indicates high official status (sometimes as connected to the games) and appears in early Christian artwork. In Greek mythology, the golden apples of the Hesperides are associated with youth and immortality.

36. The Gate of Life was the gate through which victorious combatants or losers granted mercy exited. There may have been a third gate in some places, the Gate of Victory, but evidently not in the Carthage amphitheater.

37. The biblical Garden of Eden was located in the East.

38. The text and meaning of the second half of the sentence are uncertain.

39. It is not clear whether they asked the angels or the martyrs, or whom they were asking about. The text reads literally either "And we asked them where the rest were. The angels said to us . . . " or "And we asked them where they were. The rest of the angels said to us . . . "

40. The words are in Greek as in Revelation 4:8.

41. The description of the enthroned Jesus somewhat resembles Revelation 1:13–15, but the feet are invisible here, not made of bronze.

42. Jesus is possibly wiping away tears, as promised in Revelation 7:17.

43. The kiss of peace is given at special Christian observances, such as the Sunday upright prayers of joy.

44. See note 14, above.

45. The word he uses is *papa*, from which we have "pope," the bishop of Rome. Perpetua uses the formal *pater* for her father, while Saturus gives the church official the term of endearment, which was already current among Christians.

46. The ancient sense of burnt sacrifice, including of incense and other inedible substances, was that the rising smoke nourished the gods above.

47. Secundulus, one of the original group of prisoners, may have been beheaded in prison. Luke 2:35 refers to a sword piercing Mary's soul as well as Jesus's.

48. By a modern count, Felicitas was *seven* months pregnant, but inclusive reckoning was used for such units of time, making a normal pregnancy "ten months long."

49. Recall that at 10.15 Perpetua handed over the narrative to someone else.

50. My translation for the ritual feast given to gladiators before their ordeal is approximate; it is not certain what "free" means in this connection. The ritual shared meal at the Christian assembly was the prototype of the eucharist rite.

51. The "all-important day" is Judgment Day.

52. Conventionally, the stars of the opening procession were local dignitaries, not condemned persons about to be executed.

53. The second baptism, by blood, is a commonplace of martyrdom.

54. Volunteer gladiators (as opposed to those who were slaves, prisoners of war, or criminals turned over to gladiatorial schools) had contracts, "giving themselves over" to trainers as conditional slaves.

55. The gauntlet is associated with the scourging of Jesus: see Mark 15:15, Matthew 27:26, John 19:1.

56. Assurance about divine responsiveness of this kind appears a number of times in the New Testament.

57. Victims for the beasts were displayed and immobilized on raised structures akin to stages, carts, or scaffolding.

58. I do not know of the use of a cow as an attack animal, even against women, in any other account of Roman games.

59. "Female martyr" (*martyra*) is the first known word to distinguish a martyr by her sex. It was customary for women in mourning to appear with loose, disheveled hair and sometimes to tear at it and disfigure themselves in other ways.

60. Normally only gladiators had a chance to exit through the Gate of Life, if they either won their fights or were granted clemency.

61. The crowd gives the habitual taunt, parodying a common courtesy, of a combatant bleeding profusely. The narrators echoes it, remarking literally, "He was saved/healthy who had washed in this way."

62. This is my effort to reflect a jingle in the Latin: *non conturbent sed confirment*, for "let [these things] not disturb but make solid/strong."

63. The "place of plunder," where defeated gladiators were stripped of their equipment, was also the place for administering the coup de grâce; the bodies were dragged out through the Gate of Death.

64. The text has the same wordplay on *sustineo* here as explained in note 17, above, but I have rendered it differently in English.

65. Throat-cutting was part of gladiatorial training.

66. The devil, always pictured as the inspiration behind persecutions, is here shown acting through the gladiator.

67. As in the redactor's introduction, there seems to be explicit promotion of the New Prophecy or Montanist point of view.

Index

Acts of Paul and Thecla, 49–54
Acts of Perpetua and Felicitas, 135, 138; *Acta A*, 138–139; *Acta B*, 139–140
Aeneid (Vergil), 50–51
Africa Proconsularis, 16
Agatha (martyr), 2
Agnes (martyr), 2
Agrippina the Younger, 15
Andromeda, 135
angels, 2, 76–77, 85, 93, 98–100, 103, 141, 163–165, 183n39
Apasius, 164
apocalypse, 34, 60, 63
Apocalypse of Peter, 61, 77, 87
apostolic fathers, 61, 100. *See also* church fathers
Apuleius, 59, 110
arena games, 107–117; Christians in, 107–117, 121–133, 165–169; spectators, 53, 72–73, 105, 109, 112, 113, 125, 130, 133, 167–168, 169, 170; wild animals in, 53, 110–112, 113, 125–126, 128, 129, 139, 153, 162, 165–166, 168–169, 184n58. *See also* gladiators
Arria, 133
Artaxius, 164
Augustan History, 37
Augustine of Hippo, 121; conflicted sexual urges, 142; sermons about Perpetua and Felicitas, xiv, 3, 13, 140–143, 149–150, 151
Aurelianus, Lucius Marius Maximus Perpetuus, 12
Austen, Jane, 79

baptism, 4, 11, 43, 66; authority over, 89; candidates for, 12, 34, 38, 84, 126, 128, 156, 169; of Dinocrates, 63, 89, 117, 149–150, 182n30; drink celebrating, 87, 182n20; first (by water), 53, 63, 89, 181n12, 182n30; second (by blood), 89, 124, 129, 140, 167, 169, 184n53
Basilica Maiorum (Church of the Ancestors), 13
Bible, 60–61, 66; Apocrypha, 61; Latin translations, 68, 151. *See also* Hebrew Bible; New Testament; Old Testament
Blandina, 35, 41
Bonhoeffer, Dietrich, 2
Bulwer-Lytton, Edward, 145, 180n11

Camilla, 50, 135
Caracalla (emperor), 18, 182n24
Carthage, 1, 11, 13–14, 16, 17, 33, 90, 116–117, 123, 127, 147; basilica in, 116
Catholicism, 2, 142, 151, 153
Cato the Younger, 115
celibacy, 38–40, 52. *See also* virginity
chariot racing, 38, 100, 109, 165
Christ. *See* Jesus Christ
Christianity: appeal to women, 33–34; Catholic, 2, 142, 145, 149–151, 153; celibacy fitting into early Christian society, 39–40; doctrinal controversies, 33–34; and pagan culture, 121; political defense of, 118; Protestant, 145, 151; as radical movement, 108;

Index

Christianity (*continued*)
  as threat to Roman authority, 105, 113–114
Christian literature, 3, 101
Christians: in the arena games, 109–110, 112–113, 121; persecution of, 16, 19, 115, 116; in prison, 45–46; punishment of, 18–19; purged by Diocletian, 114; in Vienne and Lyon, 19, 35, 36–37, 41, 45; in the visual arts, 136
Christie, Agatha, 116
church fathers, 3, 35, 58, 87, 100. *See also* apostolic fathers
Church History (Eusebius), 3, 19, 36
Cicero, 58
Clarke, Liz, 152–153
Cleopatra, 145
Cyprian (bishop of Carthage), 115

devil: embodiment of 85–86, 92, 95, 98, 163, 184n66; in martyr literature, 3, 37, 68, 111, 118, 119 168; Perpetua's references to, 41, 43, 66, 68, 85–86, 92, 137, 138, 157, 163, 168; victims of, 35, 37, 39
Dinocrates (brother of Perpetua): baptism of, 117, 149–150, 156, 182n30; death of, 12, 87–88; name of, 15; Perpetua's concern for, 47, 63–64, 68, 87–89, 101, 137, 160–161; Perpetua's visions of, 72, 88–90, 101, 160–162; in purgatory, 63, 72, 88, 149, 182n30
Diocletian, 114
divorce, 21–22
Donatists, 141
dreams: biblical, 82, 102; climbing/flying, 85; conventions around, 83; Freud's interpretation of, 92, 93; of heaven, 76–78; late-arrival, 85, 94, 102–103; magical qualities of, 102–103; modern studies of, 100–101. *See also* Perpetua's visions; Saturus; visions

education: of children, 61–62; of Perpetua, 12, 24–26, 61–62, 64, 105; prolonged, 104–105; of women, 105, 145
Egypt and Egyptians, 91, 95, 97, 125, 138, 162–163, 167
Elijah (biblical), 82
Eliot, George (Mary Ann Evans), 145
English Common Law, 23
Ethiopians, 14–15
eucharist, 183n50
Eusebius, 3, 19, 36

Farina, William, 8
Felicitas, 144, 150; in *Acta B*, 139–140; in the arena, 111, 124, 125, 126, 128, 129, 132, 150, 167–169; Augustine's sermons about, 3, 13, 140–143, 149, 151; birth of baby, 2, 45, 54, 113, 139–140, 165–166, 183n48; as martyr, 124, 137; meaning of her name, 13; in *Perpetua's Journey*, 152–153; as slave, 38, 156; surrendering her baby, 72–73
Flight in Time of Persecution (Tertullian), 65
Frank, Anne, 26, 78–79
Freud, Sigmund, 92, 93
From the Founding of the City (Livy), 33
Fundanus, 31–32

Garden of Eden, 86, 183n37
Garman, Steven, 180n11
Gate of Death, 184n63
Gate of Life, 88, 92, 98, 126, 128, 150, 163, 169, 183n36, 184n60

Index

Gate of Victory, 183n36
Geta Caesar, 17, 161, 182n31
Gill, Eric, 149
gladiators, 5, 74, 75, 91, 96, 109, 110, 112, 120–121, 122, 124, 130–131, 132–133, 140, 162, 166, 167, 170, 184n60, 184n63. *See also* arena games
Greek language, 15, 25, 60–61, 62, 86, 90, 99, 100, 108, 115, 164, 181n14, 182n19, 182n29, 182n32, 183n34, 183n40
Greeks, 15

hairstyles, 127
heaven: Augustine's conception of, 141; in the New Testament, 100; Saturus's vision of, 76–78, 84, 98–100, 103–104, 137–138, 163–165. *See also* paradise; Perpetua's visions
Hebrew Bible: book of Tobit, 61; Greek translations, 60; and the New Testament, 33; prohibiting imagery, 137. *See also* Old Testament
Hilarianus, 117, 125, 159–160, 167
Hippolyta, 135
Holy Spirit, 65, 155, 157, 166, 170, 181n12
Homer, 136

iconoclasts, 137
Ignatius of Antioch, 4
imperialism, 16–17, 95
infanticide, 23, 30
intertextuality, 58
Iocundus, 164

Jacob (biblical), 82, 84–85, 181n16
Jacobus de Voragine, 144
Jesus Christ: blood of, 182n33; command to disciples, 65; depictions of, 86–87, 136; in dreams, 103; Felicitas as wife of Christ, 140; incarnation of, 135; and the Last Supper, 94; as Messiah, 62; passion and crucifixion of, 54, 125, 151, 168; Perpetua as wife of, 8, 123, 167; Perpetua's reference to, 158; Perpetua's vision of, 78; pierced by sword, 183n47; redactor's references to, 140, 156, 170; in Revelation, 87, 92–93, 183n41; Second Coming of, 115; transfiguration of, 82; visions of, 76, 97, 101
Joan of Arc, 48
Joseph (biblical), 102
Judaism, 62–63
Judgment Day, 76, 123, 137, 166, 184n51
Julius Caesar, 59, 69–70
Juvenal, 29, 30, 119

kiss of peace, 76, 97, 99, 130, 131, 170, 183n43

Latin language, 8–9, 15, 16, 19, 24, 25, 58, 59, 66, 67–68, 69–70, 71, 73, 77, 82, 90, 93, 117, 119, 127, 138, 140, 150–151, 175n1 (introduction), 181n2, 181n4, 181n10, 181n17, 181–182n18, 182n22, 182n23, 182n28, 182n33, 183n45, 184n59, 184n62, 184n64
Legenda Aurea, 144
Leonides, 147
Life of Brian (film), 110
literature: apocalyptic, 61, 77, 87; Christian, 3–4, 60–61, 101; Greek and Roman, 25, 49, 58–59, 65, 73, 97; martyr, 3–4, 54, 64, 101, 105, 107–108, 111, 131, 137–138, 144; religious, 105; women's, 78–79, 104; young people's, 104–105
Livy, 33

Index

Lucretia, 33, 115, 135
Lyon, Malcolm, 146
Lyon-Vienne letter, 19, 35, 36–37, 41, 45–46
lyric poetry, 59–60

Manichaeanism, 34
Marcella, 147, 148
Marcus Aurelius, 60
marriage, 21–22, 26, 30, 39, 40, 104–105, 147, 176n11 (chapter 2)
martyr cults, 137
martyrdom: accounts of, 3–4; conventions of, 4, 6, 48, 81, 101, 105, 131, 138; documentation of, 135; Donatist view of, 141; evaluation of by scholars, 36; as inspiration, 170; lore of, 86; opposition to, 43; paths to, 118; of Perpetua, 1, 4, 15, 26, 34, 41, 42, 48, 84, 87, 97, 137, 141, 148, 156, 182n31; popularity of, 34–35, 46, 63, 115–116; pressure for, 37, 46; and religious freedom, 148–149; as second baptism, 89, 124, 129, 140, 167, 169, 184n53; as spectacle, 4, 19, 36–37, 107–108, 115, 122–133; used for recruitment, 5, 37, 39, 115; warfare imagery of, 83; white representing, 93, 182n33. *See also* arena games
martyr literature, 3–4, 49–54, 64, 101, 105 107–108, 111, 131, 137–138, 144
martyrs: blessedness of, 118; celibate, 38, 49–55; deaths of, 1, 2, 5, 7, 12, 18, 26, 37, 98, 108, 118, 129, 132, 137, 140, 150, 170; etymology of, 108; exploitation of, 36–37, 137; female, 1, 2, 21, 34–36, 47–48, 126, 139–140, 143, 168–9, 184n59; in heaven, 77–78, 98–99, 100, 137–138; human side of, 4; imagery of, 119; as joyful, 94; from Lyon and Vienne, 19, 35, 36–37, 41, 45, 46; male, 150; modern literary, 4; myths and fairy tales about, 48, 49; prayers of, 68, 87, 139, 149, 165; as saints, 2, 7; from Scillium, 16, 35, 116, 147; self-righteousness of, 150; Tertullian's exhortation to, 94; torture of, 4, 85; voices of, 2–3
Martyrs of Carthage (Webb), 145–148
Mary (mother of Jesus), 7, 135, 136, 183n47
Meditations (Marcus Aurelius), 60
Merton, Thomas, 24
Milton, John, 66
Minucius Felix, 115
Minucius Timinianus, 160
Montanist movement, 6, 7, 21, 33, 63, 64, 141, 175n3 (introduction), 181n1, 184n67. *See also* New Prophecy movement
Moses (biblical), 82
mythology, 34, 43, 50, 97, 183n35

Nero, 115
New Prophecy movement, 6, 21, 33, 63–64, 83, 181n1, 184n67. *See also* Montanist movement
New Testament: heaven of, 100; language of, 33, 90; Pastoral Epistles, 35. *See also* Bible
New Testament books: Acts, 19, 175n3 (chapter 1), 177n7, 181n3; 1 Corinthians, 176n10, 176n11, 177n3, 177n4, 177n5; 2 Corinthians, 178n2; Gospel of John, 94, 184n55; Gospel of Luke, 177n3, 178n2, 183n47; Gospel of Mark, 184n55; Gospel of Matthew, 177n6, 178n2, 184n55; 1 John, 181n6; Revelation, 64, 87, 92–93, 95, 178n7, 178n13, 178n16,

Index

182n32, 183n40; Romans, 181n5; 1 Timothy, 176n7
North Africa, 11, 16, 90, 96, 111, 116. *See also* Carthage
North Africans, 14
Numidicus, 148

Old Testament: Apocrypha, 61; Genesis, 82, 84–85, 178n6, 181n16; Joel, 177n7, 181n3. *See also* Bible; Hebrew Bible
Optatus, 100, 164, 165
Origen, 147

paradise, 12, 15, 53, 86. *See also* heaven
Paradise Lost (Milton), 66
Paul (apostle), 21–22, 33, 34, 35, 39, 40, 62, 63, 83; in *The Acts of Paul and Thecla*, 49, 51–54
Perpetua: age of, 12, 181n9; in the arena, 48, 74–75, 108, 111, 114, 120–121, 123–133, 139, 152, 161–162, 167–170; under arrest, 12, 40–41, 47–48, 117–118, 156–157; Augustine's sermons about, xiv, 3, 140–143, 149–150, 151; at the banquet, 122, 166–167; baptism of, 42; brothers of, 30, 82, 83, 128, 157, 169, 181n15; burial of, 13–14; concern for Dinocrates, 47, 63–64, 68, 87–89, 101, 137, 160–161; contentious relationship with father, 17–19, 41–43, 65–66, 69, 71–72, 73, 119, 138, 143, 152, 156–157, 159–160, 161, 182n21; death of, 132–133, 169–170; depictions of, 136–137; diary of, xiv, 1, 12; early history, 11–12; education of, 12, 24–26, 61–62, 64, 105; family of, 12-1–24, 26–27, 156–7; in jail, 5, 43–44, 47–48, 57, 119–120, 157, 161; marriage of, 9, 12, 19–22, 23, 24, 27; martyrdom of, 1, 4, 15, 26, 41, 42, 48, 84, 87, 97, 137, 141, 148, 156, 182n31; as *matrona*, 9, 18, 19–21, 30, 181n8; as mother, 1, 6, 22–23, 26, 51, 88, 89, 117, 139, 141, 156; name of, 12–14; personality of, 6–8, 11, 55, 135–6, 141; relationship with God, 8–9; as saint, 7; scholarly bibliography of, 145–147; social status of, 15–18, 181n7; transformation in the Middle Ages, 143–144; as wife of Christ, 8, 123, 167; as writer, 2, 64–76, 78–79. *See also* Perpetua's visions
Perpetua font, 149, 153
Perpetua's baby: alternate versions of story, 144; and her family, 9, 20, 22–24, 30, 43, 44, 57, 71, 139, 159–160, 182n27; with her in jail, 22, 44–45, 71; at the judicial hearing, 46, 139, 159–160; nursed by Perpetua, 12, 16, 22, 44, 46–47, 57, 72, 156, 157, 160; status of, 22–24; weaning of, 47, 71, 160
Perpetua's father: beating of, 17, 46, 160; contentious relationship with Perpetua, 18–19, 41–43, 65, 69, 71–72, 73, 119, 138, 143, 152, 156–157, 159–160, 182n21; at the judicial hearing, 46; status of, 16–18, 116; as supportive, 8, 29–30, 62; visiting her in jail, 43, 47, 88, 119, 162
Perpetua's husband, 9, 19–24, 26–27, 41, 144, 182n27; in *Martyrs of Carthage*, 147–148
Perpetua's Journey (Rea & Clarke), 152–153
Perpetua's visions: brother's role in, 5, 82, 83, 151, 157–158; contest as gladiator, 94–98, 138, 162–163;

Index

Perpetua's visions (*continued*)
of Dinocrates, 6, 12, 47, 63, 64, 72, 87, 88–90, 160–162; first vision, 83–87, 158–159; fourth vision, 90–98, 120–121, 162–163; of heaven, 78; ladder to heaven, 37, 84–85, 97, 138, 144, 158–159, 181n16; qualities of, 8, 54, 81–83, 100–105; Saturus as guide in, 5, 8, 84–87, 138, 158; second vision, 87–89, 160–161; section 8 of diary, 46; third vision, 89–90, 120, 161–162; of the underworld, 6

Peter (apostle), 82
Peterson, Amy, 145
Petronius, 59, 110, 112
Phoenicians, 14, 15
Pliny, 114; letter on a daughter's death, 30–32; letter to Trajan, 19, 113–114
Pomponius, 47, 57, 90–91, 93–94, 157, 160, 162, 182n26
prophecy, 62–63
Protestantism, 151
Psyche, 135
Pudens, 120, 129–130, 161, 169–170
purgatory, xiii, 63, 72, 88, 149–50, 182n30

Quintus, 164

racism, 14, 95
Rea, Jennifer A., 152–153
redactor (rewrite man), 1, 2, 4, 5–6, 12, 16, 26, 33, 61, 62, 63, 64, 65, 66, 73, 78, 116, 117, 145, 150
religious communities, 24, 39–40; Augustinians, 40, 142; Franciscans, 24; Trappists, 24
religious freedom, 148–149
Revocatus, 38, 125, 156, 167, 168
rhetoric, 3, 15, 25, 34, 58, 59, 65–67, 74, 121, 142, 143, 146

Roman jails, 45, 120
Rome: and Carthage, 14, 16–17; executions in, 4; Great Fire, 115; legal system of, 19–20, 22–23; persecution of Christians by, 16, 19, 113–116, 116, 152
Rusticus, 126, 128, 169

saints: depictions of, 136; martyrs as, 2
Sappho, 59–60, 71, 145
Satires 6 (Juvenal), 29, 30
Saturninus of Carthage (martyr), 125, 144, 156, 164, 167, 168
Saturus: in *Acta A*, 138–139; in the arena, 111, 125, 167, 168; at the banquet, 75–76, 123; death of, 129–131, 132, 169–170; as guide for Perpetua's dream, 5, 84–87, 138, 158; as martyr, 36, 65, 75; verbal style, 60, 150, 183n45; vision of heaven, 1, 15, 36, 76–78, 84, 98–100, 103–104, 137–138, 163–165
Satyricon (Petronius), 59, 112
Scillium, 16, 35, 116, 147
Second Coming, 115
Secundulus, 156, 165, 183n47
Septimius Severus, 18, 37, 65, 84, 182n24, 182n31
Shepherd of Hermas, 61, 87, 94
Shewring, W. H., 149–152
snake, 85–86, 104, 142, 158, 181n16
social justice, 3
Socrates, 2
Sodom, 95
Spartacus, 144
Story of a Soul (Thérèse of Lisieux), 79
Strauss, David, 145
Suffering of the Holy Perpetua and Felicitas, 1–2; early English translation of, 8; Latin and Greek manuscripts, 16, 116–117, 135, 136, 144–145, 147;

Index

narration of, 57; new translation of, 8–9, 155–170; rewriting of, 120–121; Shewring's translation of, 149–152
Suffering of the Holy Perpetua and Felicitas, by sections: (1), 33, 65–66, 155–156; (2), 2, 12, 13, 17, 24, 30, 67, 117, 156; (3), 20, 25, 41–42, 43–45, 48, 57, 66, 90, 119, 120, 152, 156–157; (4), 37, 82, 83, 84, 141, 150–151, 157–159; (5), 17, 18, 27, 30, 41–42, 43, 73, 159; (6), 17, 46–47, 69, 71, 90, 114, 119, 159–160; (7), 47, 53, 68, 87, 88–89, 116–117, 160–161; (8), 15, 43–44, 46, 47, 53, 72, 161; (9), 47, 88, 120, 122, 161–162; (10), 68, 85, 90, 91–92, 99, 152, 162–163; (11), 36, 76, 77, 78, 84, 98, 99, 137–138, 163–164; (12), 76, 77, 84, 93, 98, 99, 127–128, 164; (13), 15, 36, 76, 84, 98, 100, 127–128, 164–165; (14), 165; (15), 45, 113, 165–166; (16), 73–74, 120, 121, 122, 166; (17), 75–76, 98, 166–167; (18), 8, 15, 75, 98, 121, 123, 124, 125, 167–168; (19), 98, 111, 125, 168; (20), 48, 53, 72–73, 88, 111, 113, 125–126, 168–169; (21), 117, 129–130, 169–170
suicide, 115, 118, 129

Tertius, 57
Tertullian, 33, 58, 68, 94, 98, 115, 137–138; *Flight in Time of Persecution,* 65; *To the Martyrs,* 46
Thecla, 49–54, 88
Thérèse of Lisieux, 79

Thuburbo Minus, 16, 116
torture, 4, 19, 35, 37, 45, 46, 85, 101, 112, 113, 148
To the Martyrs (Tertullian), 46
Trajan (emperor), 18, 19, 113, 114
Tullianum (Rome), 45

Vergil, 73, 108; *Aeneid,* 50–51
Vey, P. C., 124
Vibia Perpetua. *See* Perpetua
virginity, 2, 21, 38, 39–40, 48–54, 59; cult of, 21–22. *See also* celibacy
visions: in apocryphal literature, 61; biblical, 82–83, 84–85; of Saturus, 1, 15, 76–78, 84, 98–100, 103–104, 137–138, 163–165. *See also* dreams; Perpetua's visions

Webb, Mrs. J. B. (Annie Webb-Peploe), 145–148
widowhood, 22, 29, 40, 50
women: Augustine's view of, 141–143; as authors, 59–60, 71; challenges of, 29–33; and Christianity, 33–35, 138; as Christians, 34–36, 49, 140; in the early church, 89; education of, 25; expectations of, 11; in literature, 135–136; as martyrs, 34–35, 47–49, 184n59; in the New Prophecy movement, 63–64; as prophets, 62–63; in the Roman Empire, 15–16; social expectations of, 30–33. *See also* marriage; widowhood
women's literature, 78–79, 104
Woolf, Virginia, 61, 71